Daily Guidance

Daily Guidance

by Daisaku Ikeda

translated by George M. Williams

World Tribune Press • Los Angeles

International Standard Book Number: 0-915678-09-8
Library of Congress Catalog Card Number: 76-15936
World Tribune Press, Los Angeles, CA 90406

Foreword

I received a copy of *Daily Guidance* from our master President Ikeda on January 13, 1975, on behalf of all NSA members. On the flyleaf he wrote, "I will pray for your ever-greater glory as heroic pioneers on the two roads of study and practice."

Since then we have met many challenging situations and seemingly impassable barriers on the path toward our goal. At times even I wasn't sure which way to go next. But when I opened President Ikeda's *Daily Guidance* after morning Gongyo, I always found it exactly described the campaign of that moment, and like a perfect compass, pointed out a sure course to victory.

On July 23, for example, we faced an hour of crisis: the success or failure of our Pre-Bicentennial Blue Hawaii Convention hung in the balance. His guidance for that day read, "Today may be hard—the ascent cruelly steep—but we are sons of the Gakkai. Once more, arm in arm, let's join in strong unity and courageously march on to the fresh, green fields that await us."

Almost at the very last moment, this guidance gave us the hope, courage and confidence to unite and break through that final deadlock. Not only then but throughout the entire year, we of NSA have proven over and over that by following President Ikeda's *Daily Guidance,* there is no obstacle we cannot conquer, no battle we cannot win. No matter how black, how hopeless the situation may seem, this day-by-day encouragement from our master is like the eight o'clock morning sun that rises to dispel the mists of doubt and show us the "fresh, green fields" of victory.

We can take great pride in being able to publish an English version of *Daily Guidance* in the year of our nation's Bicentennial. I sincerely hope each NSA member will continue to use President Ikeda's guidance day by day to win in all your campaigns and realize every one of your dreams in life. Let's always remember "Hope, courage and confidence" as he taught us.

George M. Williams
General Director
July 4, 1976

January

JANUARY 1

Happy New Year to all my dear friends! I expect this will be another busy year, but nevertheless I urge you: Live for Kosen-rufu. Forge iron unity for Kosen-rufu. And persevere, day by day, for Kosen-rufu.

一月一日

親愛なるみなさま
明けましておめでとうございます
この一年も
多忙なことと思いますが
広布のために生きぬき
広布のために鉄の団結をもち
広布のために執念ある
一日一日を送ってください

President Ikeda's novel, *The Human Revolution*, first appears in *Seikyo Shinbun*, 1965. *

*Historic events on respective dates appear at the bottom of the page.

JANUARY 2

Let's take a step forward in everything.
That is the swiftest road to glory.

すべてに
一歩前進しよう
それが栄光への
最直道である

一月二日

Third President Daisaku Ikeda born, 1928.

JANUARY 3

To stay healthy and make sound progress day after day, you must do morning and evening Gongyo consistently.

一月三日

ともかく
くる日もくる日も健康で
逞しい建設を
するために
五座三座の勤行を
やりぬくことだ

JANUARY 4

Now is the time to develop ourselves, improve our lives and build our organization. Then, let's advance together, youthfully and courageously, in the great task of building Kosen-rufu.

一月四日

さあ
自己の建設に
生活の建設に
組織の建設に
そして広布への偉大なる建設に
勇敢に若々しく
ともに前進していこう

JANUARY 5

Make a habit of reading the Gosho, even if it's just a single passage. Never forget that the Gosho embodies the prime point of 'faith equals society.'

一月五日

一節でもいいから
御書を読む習慣をつけよう
そこに信心即社会の
原点のあることを
けっして忘れてはならない

JANUARY 6

This year, let's not have a single accident.
This year, let's perfect our organization through discussion meetings.
This year, let's thoroughly check over and improve everything and take good care of our own areas of responsibility.

一　月　六　日

この一年
絶対に事故のないようにしよう
この一年
座談会で組織を完璧にしよう
この一年
すべてを総点検し総開発しよう
それぞれの社会を大切にしながら

President Ikeda leaves for U.S. and Guam, 1975.

Life is long — no matter what happens, don't be impatient. Be confident that the road you tread will surely lead you to a victory without regrets.

長い人生である——

何があっても焦らず

かならず自分自身は悔いない

勝利への帰着の道を

歩んでいることを

確信することだ

一月七日

JANUARY 8

Let's do Gongyo intently without rushing.
Let's discuss our plans fully and give thorough
guidance. Then, let's forge ahead gallantly in
our battle to build.

一
月
八
日

そ じ じ じ
し っ っ っ
て く く く
　 り り り
　 指 打 勤
建 導 ち 行
設 し 合 し
へ よ わ よ
の う せ う
戦 　 し
い 　 よ
を 　 う

堂
々
と
進
め
て
い
こ
う

President Ikeda leaves for U.S., France, Switzerland, Italy, Lebanon,
India and Hong Kong, 1963.

JANUARY 9

Leaders must never be arrogant. Let's talk with everyone and show them warm understanding.

幹部は絶対に
威張ってはいけない
すべての人を
あたたかく包容し
話し合おう

一
月
九
日

Second All America General Meeting, Los Angeles, 1965.
President Ikeda dedicates new New York Community Center, 1975.

JANUARY 10

First, chant resounding Daimoku with the confidence that your prayers will be answered. Then, take time to talk with your juniors and hear all that they have to say.

一月十日

まず朗々と題目をあげよう
祈りの叶うことを確信して
そしてゆっくり後輩と語り
すべてを聞いてあげよう

JANUARY 11

Take the very best care of capable people.
That is the greatest guidance you can offer.

指導であるからだ
それが最大の
大切にしよう
人材を最高に

一月十一日

International premiere of *The Human Revolution* film, Los Angeles, 1974.

JANUARY 12

We should be able to lead people at any time with masterful lectures, guidance, speeches, plans and writing.

一月十二日

われわれはいかなる時でも

名講義

名指導

名演説

名企画

名文をもって

人々をリードしていくべきだ

JANUARY 13

Let's do our best to work with all kinds of people, irrespective of position. Let's encourage and assist them warmly and kindly; after all, we are brothers and sisters from the eternal past.

一月十三日

いかなる人に対しても
最善を尽くし接していこう
役職のいかんを問わず
親切にあたたかく応援し
激励していくべきだ
所詮は久遠よりの
兄弟であるからだ

You participate in discussion meetings first and then encourage other people to do the same. Through this steady, basic effort you can take a firm step forward in the true practice of Buddhism (Nyosetsu Shugyo).

まず自ら座談会に参加しよう
そして参加させよう
この地道にして
身近なところに
真実の如説修行の
厳たる一歩があるからだ

一月十四日

Hawaii Community Center Gohonzon Enshrining Ceremony, President Ikeda attending, 1966.

JANUARY 15

Let's live proudly, as sons of the lion king. Awaken to what President Toda stated in his Precepts for Youth: 'It is a disgrace for a true disciple to be praised by fools, but to be praised by Nichiren Daishonin is the greatest honor in life.'

一月十五日

師子の子は
誇り高く生きぬこう
愚人にほむらるるは
智者の恥辱なり
大聖にほむらるるは
一生の名誉なりの自覚で

JANUARY 16

Face the morning in high spirits, and the whole day will be off to a good start.

朝は元気で
一日の出発なれば

一月十六日

President Ikeda dedicates Chicago Community Center, 1975.

JANUARY 17

Do your work quickly yet well. Use your spare time effectively to plan ahead so that your next move can be both bold and accurate.

一月十七日

仕事は早く
しかも立派にやろう
そして残った時間を有効に
次への計画にあてよう
正確に かつ大胆に
次の行動をなすために

JANUARY 18

Never exhaust yourself through lack of sleep. The important thing is to carry on steady and productive campaigns.

進めていくことだ

順調に価値的な戦いを

寝不足して疲れてはならぬ

けっして

一月十八日

JANUARY 19

Now is the time to accelerate your engine for this year's undertakings. That means to chant Daimoku until you feel satisfied. Strive again today, freely and powerfully.

一月十九日

さあ
一年間の建設のために
エンジンをフル回転させよう
それは心豊かな題目だ
今日も伸びのびと逞しく

28

JANUARY 20

*Let's make a point of reaching today's
goal today. That is the cause for an enjoyable
victory in tomorrow's campaign.*

一月二十日

今日の目標は
今日のうちに
かならず達成しよう
それがまた
明日の戦いへの
楽しい勝利の因であるからだ

JANUARY 21

Never be conceited or intoxicated by your own success. The moment you do, your progress grinds to a halt. Let's advance continually with a youthful, seeking spirit.

一月二十一日

けっして
有頂天になるな
うぬぼれてはならぬ
その時から
前進がとまってしまうからだ
常に若々しい
求道者として進もう

JANUARY 22

Don't be swayed by temporary ups and downs. Without the least hesitation, advance in bold array.

一喜一憂するな
なにごとも遠慮せず
堂々たる体勢で
進みゆけ

一月二十二日

Ashuzan Myosenji Temple opens, Washington D.C., 1972.

JANUARY 23

Wherever we go, let's always show number one results. This requires detailed planning, powerful action and guidance based on understanding people's hearts.

一月二十三日

われわれのゆくところ

常に第一位の成果を示そう

そのためには

計画の緻密さ

逞しい実行力

その人の心になりきっての

指導が大切だ

JANUARY 24

Let's stride boldly through life, cherishing high hopes, and continually chant Daimoku. Absolutely nothing is more powerful than Daimoku.

希望高らかに
題目を唱えきって
人生を闊歩しよう
題目に勝るものは
絶対にないからだ

一月二十四日

*Let's pave our own way with dignity,
ignoring criticism and slander. Let's maintain
our iron unity and our confidence in the strict
law of Buddhism.*

一月二十五日

批判中傷など
歯牙にもかけず
わが道を堂々と切り拓こう
鉄の団結と
仏法の厳しさを
確信して

JANUARY 26

When the worst happens, the best is soon to come. As leaders, let's take command gallantly and cheerfully, convinced that absolutely nothing can destroy our faith.

大悪起これば大善来る

幹部は朗らかにさっそうと

指揮をとろう

信心はなにものにも

絶対に壊されるものではない

一月二十六日

First IBL World Peace Conference held in Guam; President Ikeda inaugurated IBL Chairman, President of Soka Gakkai International, 1975.

JANUARY 27

Regard this moment as your chance to build. Quietly, yet deeply and extensively, advance and expand on every front.

一月二十七日

静かに深く　そして広く

あらゆる場面に

拡大前進しゆく

今を構築のチャンスと

心得ることだ

JANUARY 28

With renewed spirit, let's promote the spread of Buddhism and the steady development of capable people. Let's use good common sense and allow absolutely no accidents.

一月二十八日

新生の息吹（いぶき）高らかに
着実な人材育成と
仏法拡大を推進しよう
常識豊かに
絶対事故をおこさず

President Ikeda leaves for Hong Kong, Sri Lanka (Ceylon), India, Burma, Thailand and Cambodia, 1961.

JANUARY 29

Accomplish your mission for today. That is your road to victory.

今日の
使命を果たせ
汝の
勝利への道として

一月二十九日

President Ikeda leaves for Iran, Iraq, Turkey, Greece, Egypt, Pakistan and Hong Kong, 1962.

JANUARY 30

Protect each of your members and take time to talk with them. Be broad-minded, uphold the Gakkai spirit and burn with supreme conviction.

一月三十日

ともかく一人ひとりの会員を
だき抱えながら
じっくり懇談をしていこう
大確信に燃えた学会精神と
包容力をもって

JANUARY 31

Human beings are governed by emotion,
so be careful how you talk to people. You can
either awaken a seeking spirit in a great many
individuals or turn them away altogether,
depending upon your manner of speech.

一月三十一日

人間は感情に

支配されるものであるがゆえに

言葉遣いには気をつけよう

言葉遣いのいかんによって

多くの人が求道にも立つし

反対に　去り行く人にも

なってしまうからだ

February

FEBRUARY 1

February's here, our traditional month of Shakubuku. Let's strengthen our bodies, our faith and our organization this month, and open unlimited possibilities.

二月一日

さあ
伝統の二月だ
この一か月鍛えよう
信心も身体も組織も
そして限りない可能性を
開ききろう

FEBRUARY 2

Remember that your actions as a single individual will influence everyone around you.

二
月
二
日

自分一人の
行動の姿が
周りの人のすべてに
影響を与えることを
忘れるな

FEBRUARY 3

Let's work together,
enjoy ourselves together
and prosper together.

二月三日

みんなで働き
みんなで楽しみ
みんなで栄えよう

FEBRUARY 4

*To live the day cheerfully with your
purpose clear in mind, do morning Gongyo
with undivided attention.*

二
月

四
日

今日一日を明確に
そして今日一日を
朗らかに生きゆくために
朝の勤行を
悠然としぬくことだ

45

FEBRUARY 5

Once you realize that ultimately, nobody but you is to blame, you have perceived the true nature of reality. Remember that this awakening is the first step in your human revolution.

だれのせいでもない

結局　自分なのだと

自覚したときが

如実知見である

人間革命の第一歩は

そこから始まることを

忘れまい

FEBRUARY 6

As leaders, don't be arrogant, lose your temper or complain. Take the lead with the guts that come from faith and be consistently warm and understanding toward everyone.

二月六日

幹部はいばるな
怒るな　嘆くな
あくまでも
信心の根性をもって
すべてをあたたかく包容し
指揮をとろう

FEBRUARY 7

Our bodies are our most important possession, so let's take care of our health in every way possible. Continued good health is the wellspring of our activities for Kosen-rufu. We should also make our homes safe against fires and other accidents.

二月七日

お互いにもっとも大切な身体である

ゆえに　あらゆる方法をもって

健康に注意せねばならぬ

その持続が広宣流布の

活動の源泉である

共に　家庭も絶対に

火災などおこさない

安泰なものとせねばならない

FEBRUARY 8

Don't ever forget that if you think you can breeze through life just because you practice, you're taking your faith for granted. When that happens, you can't create any value at all from day to day and you'll lose your bearings.

二月八日

信心しているからといって
心に生活のスキをつくることは
信心への甘えであることを
けっして忘れてはならない
それでは何らの生活の価値も
創造できないし
乱れていこう

FEBRUARY 9

In life, you must always be awake and ready for anything, but don't exhaust yourself for long periods of time. Your actions won't be productive when you're overtired.

二月九日

人生いつも
張りは必要であるが
けっして疲労が
続いてはならない
疲労の行動のなかには
価値ある結果は
生まれないからだ

FEBRUARY 10

Leaders should cut their planning meetings, conferences and paper work to an absolute minimum. You should be fighting on the front lines — discussion meetings and individual guidance. These are the real foundation of the Gakkai. Pointless conferences are a waste of time and amount to no more than escape.

二月十日

幹部は協議　会議　事務書類を

最少限度に縮少して

座談会に　後輩の一対一の指導にと

学会の根本ともいうべき

第一線に立つべきだ

焦点なき会議は

空転であり逃避である

The man who lives up to his beliefs and practices just as the True Buddha taught (Nyosetsu Shugyo) should advance yet again today, proud as the sun, in developing capable people who are strong yet kindhearted.

二月十一日

ともかく
信条のままに生きぬく
如説修行者は
今日も太陽のごとく胸を張り
強くして優しき人材建設に
進みゆくことだ

Second President Josei Toda born, 1900.

FEBRUARY 12

Win friends.
Develop yourself.
Build a castle of capable men.

味方をつくれ
自分をつくれ
さらに力ある
人材の城をつくれ

二月十二日

FEBRUARY 13

We are sons of the Gakkai. Fearing nothing, let's unite and advance resolutely in the cause of justice.

二月十三日

われらは学会っ子だ
なにごとも恐れずに
正義のために
強気でいこう
それぞれ団結して

FEBRUARY 14

Gloom and fatigue are causes of defeat.
Growth and cheerfulness are causes for victory.

暗い疲労は
敗北の因
明るい成長は
勝利の因

二月十四日

FEBRUARY 15

What is our purpose? What is your goal today? Keeping these targets clear in mind will make for productive and worthwhile activities.

二月十五日

われわれの目的は何か
今日の目的は何かを
明確にすることだ
そこに無駄のない
価値ある活動が生まれよう

Mexico Headquarters Gohonzon Enshrining Ceremony, 1970.

FEBRUARY 16

Return to the Gakkai spirit.

学会精神に
立ち戻れ

二月十六日

Nichiren Daishonin born, 1222.

FEBRUARY 17

Let's put our full effort, based upon Gongyo, into developing individuals, thereby building a solid foundation for the Gakkai. Act positively, with the determination to have each member participate.

二月十七日

勤行を根本に
一人ひとりの構築に
総力をあげよう
これが
学会磐石の基盤をつくる源泉だ
全員参加の精神で
積極的に行動しよう

FEBRUARY 18

Recognize devils for what they are and coolly challenge them, confident of the power of the supreme Law.

魔を魔と見破って
悠然と挑もう
妙法の力を
確信して

二月十八日

FEBRUARY 19

Think over each task the day before. That is the basis of all victories.

二月十九日

一つ一つの仕事を
前日によく思索しよう
それが一切の
勝利の基なれば

FEBRUARY 20

Tackle situations with self-confidence.

自信を持って
事に処せ

二月二十日

FEBRUARY 21

First of all, let's talk over any problems together, irrespective of position, and communicate effectively. This will make our activities smooth and enjoyable.

まず上下の差別なく
なんでも相談しよう
そして連絡をとりあおう
そこにこそスムーズで
気持ちよい活動が
生まれるからだ

二月二十一日

FEBRUARY 22

*Let's take our stand in the midst of the
public and courageously open up a golden road.
That is the true image of a Gakkai leader.*

二月二十二日

民衆の真っただなかにはいって

黄金の道を勇敢に

拓いていこう

これが真の学会幹部だ

*Exert your utmost in defending the post
assigned to you, and you will definitely be
laying a foundation for growth and victory.*

二月二十三日

与えられたわが部署は
完璧に守りきろう
それがかならず
勝利と発展への
基盤となるからだ

FEBRUARY 24

Enjoy your day with good health and self-assurance.

今日も健康で
そして
余裕ある一日を

二月二十四日

FEBRUARY 25

Let's face the icy north wind with a refreshed seeking spirit (Kyudoshin). Above all, let's unite cheerfully and vigorously.

二月二十五日

すがすがしい求道心で
北風に向かおう
第一にも第二にも
明るく逞しく
スクラムを組んで

FEBRUARY 26

Let's go to bed early to refresh ourselves physically and mentally for the next day's activities. Let's keep steadily blazing a trail toward victory.

明日の活力のために
早く休み　心身を整え
常に悠然と勝利の道を
切り開こう

二月二十六日

FEBRUARY 27

Let's take common-sense action and give common-sense guidance, showing respect for our neighbors and society. That is the 'golden mean' of Myoho.

常識豊かな行動をとろう

常識豊かな指導をしよう

これが妙法の中道主義である

社会　隣人を大切にしながら

二月二十七日

FEBRUARY 28

Let's especially protect and encourage our friends whose parents don't practice or whose husbands don't share their faith.

両親の信心してない友を
夫に信心のない人を
とくに護り
励ましていこう

二月二十八日

FEBRUARY 29

*Let's further deepen our friendship with
our neighbors and respect the community,
steadily paving the way to a new era.*

二月二十九日

近隣との友好をさらに深め

そして社会を

大切にしながら

新しい時代の路線を

堅実に築き開こう

March

MARCH 1

March is here, the month when flowers blossom. Let's refresh our Gongyo this month so we can start on our human revolution and spread Buddhism courageously.

三月一日

花咲く三月
この一か月間
清々しい勤行で
人間革命と
勇気ある仏法拡大を
開始しよう

MARCH 2

Leaders should choose their words carefully when talking to their juniors, since courtesy among members serves as excellent guidance.

三月二日

幹部は言葉遣いに
じゅうぶん注意して
後輩に接しよう
同志間の礼儀が
立派な
指導となるからだ

MARCH 3

Let's face up to the harsh realities of society. Its deadlocks are broken by the power of faith. Stop looking for an easy way out.

厳しい社会の現実を
直視しよう
その打開が信心の力である
甘い考えは断じて
捨てることだ

三月三日

MARCH 4

Let's strengthen the castle and outer walls of Kokudo Seken, the place where we live and work.

わが常住する国土世間の

城壁と本丸を

堅固につくりあげよう

三月四日

MARCH 5

Brilliant plans, unity founded on mutual trust, steady results and undeniable proof all require Daimoku and strong vitality.

三月五日

聡明なる企画
信頼の団結
着実なる成果
厳然たる証拠
それには
題目と生命力で

MARCH 6

Never be daunted in your activities for Kosen-rufu. If one person falls behind, we'll muster a thousand more who will fight beside us.

三　月　六　日

広布の活動においては
断じて臆してはならぬ
たとえ一人の
退転者があっても
千人の味方を
つくろうではないか

President Ikeda leaves for Brazil, Peru and U.S., 1966.

MARCH 7

Sleep is definitely necessary to keep up our activities. Not until we can function vigorously morning, noon and night can we create real value.

三月七日

活動しゆくための源泉は
なんといっても
睡眠をとることだ
朝も昼も夜も
生き生きと動くところに
初めて価値が
生まれるのだ

President Ikeda leaves for U.S., Panama and Peru, 1974.

MARCH 8

Let's hold bright, successful discussion meetings where every single person feels he has gained something. A succession of such meetings, though small in scale, will swell to form the vast ocean of Kosen-rufu.

三月 八日

明朗な会合をしよう
充実した会合をひらこう
そして一人ももれなく
価値を感ずる会合にしよう
小さくともその集積が
偉大な広布の大海と
なっていくからだ

MARCH 9

Unite cheerfully on every front and achieve maximum results, both for your own sake and for others in society.

各部署で
明るく団結せよ
そして自己のため
隣人のため
最大の効果をあげよう

三月九日

President Ikeda dedicates San Francisco Community Center, 1974.

*The Lotus Sutra reads, 'There is great
hostility (against Buddhism) even in the
Buddha's lifetime; there will be still greater
after his death.' Let's be fully aware of this and
forge on together with great pride as sons of the
Gakkai. 'Don the robe of gentleness and
forbearance' and win the trust of society,
confident that such is the true practice
of Buddhism.*

猶多怨嫉の経文を色読し

ともどもに

学会っ子の誇りも高く進もう

また柔和忍辱の衣を着て

社会の信用を勝ちとろう

それが本門の仏道修行と

確信して

三月十日

MARCH 11

Let's study the Gosho and pray with absolute conviction, so we can grasp everything in the light of its teachings.

三月十一日

御書を拝読しよう

御書のうえから

一切をみきわめていこう

絶対の祈りで

MARCH 12

Let's work hard at our jobs, respect our neighbors and take good care of our fellow members. That way we can sink strong, deep roots in society.

三月十二日

職場を大事にしよう
隣人を大事にしよう
同志を大事にしよう
それが社会に深く強く
根を張ることだ

MARCH 13

First, have confidence. Second, have con-
fidence. Third, have confidence. And make
sound, cheerful progress in everything.

第一にも確信

第二にも確信

第三にも確信をもって

朗らかに逞しく

すべてを建設していこう

三月十三日

MARCH 14

Let's take the initiative in discussion meet-
ings, and develop them cheerfully and vigor-
ously.

三月十四日

座談会に
率先して出よう
そして楽しく逞しく
盛り上げていこう

Discussion meetings are the power source that enables everyone to fight with self-confidence. Let's drop formality and cut out any waste of time or effort. It is the Gakkai tradition for all members to participate.

三月十五日

会合は皆が
自信をもって戦えるための
電源である
形式をやめ
ムダをはぶこう
全員参加が学会の伝統だ

MARCH 16

Today is March 16. Let's start again from today and challenge everything in unity. No matter what, let's advance with bold steps toward overwhelming victory, aiming at next March 16.

三月十六日

今日は三月十六日
この日を再び第一歩として
あらゆるものに
団結で挑戦をしながら
来年の三月十六日を目標に
堂々たる大勝利の歩を
かならず進めよう

Kosen-rufu Commemorative Ceremony, 1958.
Santo Domingo Community Center opens, 1976.

MARCH 17

Buddhism is reason. Don't go to extremes or force others against their will. Let's expand our circle of friendship by forming ties of trust and sincerity.

三月十七日

仏法は道理である

無理や強引はいけない

誠意と信頼のきずなで

友人との

連帯の輪を広げよう

MARCH 18

Don't baby yourself or take advantage of society or your surroundings. A spoiled attitude shows your faith is deteriorating. All progress is based on the law of strict self-discipline.

三月十八日

自分に甘えるな
社会に甘えるな
環境に甘えるな
甘えは信心の堕落だ
自己を律する厳しさが
一切を向上に結びつける
法則なのだ

*Common-sense actions and cheerful ac-
tivities will open the way to Kosen-rufu. Sense-
less actions amount to fanaticism and are devils
which destroy our harmonious unity (Wagoso).
You should take care to avoid this.*

常識の行動と
朗らかな活動のところに
広宣流布の開拓は生まれる
非常識な行動は狂信であり
和合僧を破壊する魔であり
警戒しなくてはならぬ

三月十九日

President Ikeda presides over reorganization of America Headquarters, 1966.

MARCH 20

All kinds of obstacles will arise on the journey towards Kosen-rufu. But we, yielding to nothing, will change poison into medicine (Hendoku Iyaku) and once again, forge on courageously.

三月二十日

広宣流布への道程にあっては
さまざまな障礙も
出来するであろう
しかしわれらは
なにものにも屈せず
変毒為薬の堂々たる前進を
繰り返していくことだ

Gakkai members are Bodhisattvas of the Earth. Let's devise all kinds of ways to raise, polish and protect each of them. Be confident that even one such individual will profoundly influence five or ten more.

三月二十一日

ともかく

あらゆる方法を講じて

一人ひとりの

地涌の菩薩の学会員を

磨き　守り　育てよう

その一人が五人十人に

大きな波動を与えることを

確信しながら

MARCH 22

Without fail, let's take another step toward our next target, armed with new plans and new resolutions. Let's unite staunchly and help and encourage each other as friends from the eternal past.

次の目標を目指し
新しい決意と計画のもとに
かならずや一歩前進しよう
久遠よりの友として
励ましあい助けあいながら
強く強くスクラム組んで

三月二十二日

MARCH 23

We must advance yet another step today,
so get plenty of rest and challenge everything
with brimming vitality.

三月二十三日

われらはきょうも
一歩前進しなくてはならない
そのために
十分な休息をとりながら
生命力を満々とたたえ
すべてに挑戦していくことだ

MARCH 24

Let's climb the slopes of spring together in harmony and good will. Even one personal accident can damage Kosen-rufu and is totally against the teachings of Buddhism.

三月二十四日

春の坂を仲良く
善意に満ちて前進しよう
もはや一人たりとも
事故を起こすことは
広宣流布を傷つける
大謗法である

MARCH 25

Remember the Gakkai spirit.
Remember it is an honor to be children of the Gakkai.
Remember the Gakkai itself is the core of everything.

学会精神を忘れるな
学会っ子の栄誉を忘れるな
学会こそ
一切の中核たることを
忘れるな

三月二十五日

MARCH 26

No matter how busy you are, clearly map out your next target during morning and evening Gongyo and Daimoku. That way you can avoid any loss of initiative or fruitless effort.

三月二十六日

たとえ
いかに多忙であっても
朝な夕なの唱題のなかで
次の目標を明確に
思索することだ
一切の空転と受身を
排するために

MARCH 27

Protect and care for one individual and raise him to be a courageous man of practice. Focusing your efforts in this direction is an immediate step toward Kosen-rufu.

一人を守り
大切にすることだ
一人を勇気ある
実践者にすることだ
そこに鋭く
焦点をおくことが
身近な広宣流布の一歩である

三月二十七日

MARCH 28

Unity is the cause for all victories — this is an eternal truth. Let's strengthen our ties with each individual and persevere in our activities of social justice.

すべての勝因が

団結にあることは

永久の真理だ

ともかく

一人ひとりの絆を見事に深め

社会正義の活動を

執念をもって進めよう

三月二十八日

MARCH 29

Let's value ourselves, our families and our places of work. Toward these ends, we should value our faith.

三月二十九日

自分自身を大切にしよう
家庭を大切にしよう
職場を大切にしよう
そのために
信心を大切にしよう

MARCH 30

Buddhism is a battle against devils and obstacles. You can defeat them only with the power of strong Daimoku. Accidents show you've been defeated by devils, so you should take a strict look at yourself.

三月三十日

仏法は魔との勝負である
それを勝ち伏せていくのは
強盛なる題目の力以外にない
事故は魔に負けた証拠であると
厳しく反省すべきだ

MARCH 31

Let's set a definite time when meetings will begin and end. Meetings run haphazardly will stagnate and be unproductive.

三月三十一日

会合の初めと
終わりの時間は
明確にしよう
節度なき運営は
惰性となり
無価値になるからだ

President Ikeda opens Santa Ana Community Center, 1974.

April

APRIL 1

*Now it is April, the month of blossoms.
Let's grow, brimming with hope, and advance
one step in everything. To create hope, live with
hope and fulfill our hopes—that's faith.*

四月一日

さあ　花の四月だ
希望にみちて
すべてに一歩前進しよう
成長しよう
希望をつくり
希望に生き
希望を実現することが
信心だ

President Ikeda lectures at UCLA, 1974.

APRIL 2

*In that land or this region, the courageous
leaders of Buddhism strive hard and flourish.
Let's send Daimoku to our friends throughout
the world and make sure we ourselves don't fall
behind.*

四
月
二
日

あ
の
地
で
も

こ
の
地
で
も

勇
気
あ
る
仏
法
リ
ー
ダ
ー
は

乱
舞
し
て
い
る

日
本
の
わ
れ
わ
れ
も
遅
れ
ま
い

そ
し
て
世
界
の
同
志
に
も

題
目
を
送
ろ
う

Second President Josei Toda dies, 1958.
First America Fife and Drum Corps Recital, 1967.

APRIL 3

Be warm and considerate to those whose homes are used for discussion meetings. A show of sincere appreciation on your part will be a model of the Buddhist family.

四月三日

拠点の会場には
あたたかい心づかいをしていこう
真心をもって報いるなかに
仏法家族の
縮図があるからだ

APRIL 4

Never cause accidents. Mothers especially should keep a close eye on their children. Living each day serenely and without mishap is the image of a Gakkai member.

四月四日

絶対に事故は起こすな

とくに母親は

子供の安全に

細心の注意をはらおう

日々　安穏無事が

信仰者の姿である

APRIL 5

Leaders who don't do Gongyo aren't qualified to be leaders. People who cause trouble for others in society aren't even qualified to be members.

四
月
五
日

勤行をしない幹部は・
幹部の資格がない
そして社会に
迷惑をかけるような人は
会員の資格が
まったくない

President Ikeda dedicates San Diego Community Center, 1974.

APRIL 6

If you're not advancing, you're falling behind. If you're not fighting, you're already defeated. In Buddhism there is no middle ground. Realize that practicing for others' happiness is the first step in our battle for glory.

進まざるは退転

戦わざるも　また敗北

仏法に中間はない

ともかく利他の実践こそ

栄光への戦いの

第一歩と知れ

四月六日

APRIL 7

Persist in your own efforts rather than pressuring others. Pressure never yields positive results. Persistence shows your confident faith and will never fail to move people's hearts.

四
月
七
日

押しつけと粘りは異なる

押しつけは

百害あって一利なく

粘りは

確信ある信心のあらわれであり

かならず人の心を

動かすものである

San Diego/Mexico Convention — 11th NSA General Meeting held in San Diego, President Ikeda attending, 1974.

APRIL 8

Daimoku is the fundamental power of the Gakkai. It is an absolute, unrivaled weapon. Adjusting to society is also important, but don't lose sight of your faith in doing so.

学会の本源力は
唱題である
他にはない絶対の武器である
社会に融合することも
大切であるが
そのために信心を
見失ってはならない

四月八日

APRIL 9

Those who neglect daily Gongyo will be spiritless and tend to have many accidents. The Gosho states, 'Exert yourself in the two ways of practice and study.' Those who steadfastly uphold and practice this teaching will definitely have everything they desire by the time they reach their ultimate goal in life.

四月九日

ともかく
毎日の勤行をしない人に
歓喜なく事故が多い
〝行学の二道をはげみ候べし〟の
御金言を忍耐強く
持続　実践する人こそ
人生の総仕上げの時に
所願満足は疑いないのだ

APRIL 10

It is the ultimate disgrace for a man of principles to be swayed by criticism or slander — even worse, for a believer in true Buddhism.

四月十日

批判中傷をうけて
紛動されるということは
主義主張に生きる者として
いわんや
信仰者にとって
最大の恥である

APRIL 11

*Each of you should establish yourself,
prosper and be the winner in your own society.
That is the real campaign.*

己が社会に根を張り

己が社会で栄え

そして

己が社会で勝て

これが真実の闘争だ

四月十一日

APRIL 12

Spring is here. Let's carry out a practice full of youthful hopes and advance in a dynamic rhythm.

四月十二日

さあ春だ
われらも青春のごとき
希望に満ちた信心をしよう
そして躍動する
リズムに乗って
前進だ

APRIL 13

Distill all your past experience for the next undertaking. That is a vital factor in building a new era.

四月十三日

経験を総括し
次の創造を
していくことだ
それが新しい時代を
構築する決め手である

APRIL 14

Read widely, write well and speak convincingly. That is the driving force of great development.

四
月
十
四
日

よく読め
よく書け
そして雄弁たれ
それが偉大なる
発展への推進力だ

President Ikeda leaves for People's Republic of China, 1975.

APRIL 15

Never go off and worry all by yourself.
Whatever the problem, talk it over with good
friends or experienced seniors.

けっして
自分だけで悩むな
よき友
よき先輩と
なんでも相談していくことだ

四月十五日

APRIL 16

'Stand alone!
'Another will definitely follow you!
'A third will then appear!'
Let's have faith in these words of our late master President Toda and forge bravely ahead to build a new era.

四月十六日

「一人立て
二人は必ず立たん
三人はまたつづくであろう」の
恩師の言を確信し
新時代の建設に
勇敢に進もう

APRIL 17

Bring out your own special qualities and give full play to your individuality. Pursue your own course with self-confidence. Then you won't feel worthless or insecure. This is the faith of Jitai Kensho, or revealing your true and highest potential.

四月十七日

自分の特質を生かせ
自分の個性を生かせ
わが道に自信をもって
進みぬくことだ
そこには不安もなく
卑屈もない
これが自体顕照の信心だ

APRIL 18

*Once you set your course, don't change it.
When a change of plans is necessary, make sure
all the members understand so they can practice cheerfully. This is a cause to advance
toward victory.*

四月十八日

決まった方針は変えるな

もし変えねばならぬ事態の時は

全員が喜んで納得するように

せねばならぬ

これが勝利への前進の因だ

APRIL 19

Let's inspire all our members to stand up and fight. Let's exercise leadership effectively so that no one gets exhausted.

四月十九日

全員が奮い立つ
激励をしよう
そして皆が疲れない
価値ある指揮をとろう

APRIL 20

*Let's read our organization's newspaper
ourselves and launch a movement to have our
members read it, too. Be confident these efforts
are a model of the whole scope of Kosen-rufu.*

四月二十日

われらの機関紙を読もう
そして
読ませる運動もしよう
そこに広宣流布の
一切の縮図があることを
確信しながら

Seikyo Shinbun publishes first issue, 1951.

APRIL 21

Leaders themselves should take the lead in visiting members at home. Be courteous but don't be hesitant. Forget about status, position or what people may think of you, and talk with your members heart to heart.

四月二十一日

家庭指導は
幹部自身が大胆(だいたん)に
最先端にいくことだ
そこには
肩書や役職　世間体を
ぬぐい捨てていくことだ

APRIL 22

The basis of all guidance in faith should be to enable everyone to carry out activities confidently and cheerfully.

四月二十二日

一切の信心指導の根本は
みんなが明るく
自信をもって
活動できるように
してあげることだ

APRIL 23

Guidance, communications and reports should be prompt and accurate. That is essential for tomorrow's growth and victory.

四月二十三日

指導　伝達　報告は

はやく正確に行うこと

それが

明日への勝利と

建設の要因であるからだ

APRIL 24

Now is the time to stand up with pure and gallant faith. As you chant more and more and still more Daimoku, you will bring out the qualities of a true child of the Gakkai and a power which commands respect.

四月二十四日

今こそ潔（いさぎよ）い信心にたとう
題目をあげてあげて
あげぬいていくところに
真の学会っ子の本領と
尊い力が湧（わ）くのだ

APRIL 25

Size up situations with unerring judgment. Remember that great conviction must be based on cool intellect, and reason should stem from great passion.

四月二十五日

すべてのことに
情勢分析を誤るな
知性のうえの大確信
大情熱のうえの理性を
忘れるな

APRIL 26

Let's pray for our friends and then open our hearts to them. That is the only real Buddhist movement.

四月二十六日

ともかく
わが友のために祈ろう
そしてわが友と対話しぬこう
そのなかにしか
確たる仏法運動はないからだ

APRIL 27

Be brave, calm and wise.

勇敢たれ
沈着たれ
賢明たれ

四月二十七日

APRIL 28

Let's fight again today, aglow with life-force like the eight o'clock morning sun, while at the same time, showing respect for society.

午前八時の太陽のごとき
生命力で
今日一日も戦おう
社会を大切にしながら

四月二十八日

Nichiren Daishonin establishes true Buddhism, 1253.

To avoid failures, let's take time to discuss things thoroughly before we act. Since 'faith equals society,' we must not cause any accidents or mishaps.

四月二十九日

絶対に失敗のないように
事前の協議を
じっくりやって
行動に移そう
いかなる事件も事故も
起こしてはならぬ
信心即社会なれば

President Ikeda leaves for France, England and U.S., 1972.

APRIL 30

Don't mistreat yourself, because your life is precious for Kosen-rufu.

自分を粗末にするな
広布の大事な
生命なれば

四月三十日

May

MAY 1

Leaders must always be courteous. When you explain Buddhism to people, show firm confidence in both your words and actions. Furthermore, in the revolution of Kosen-rufu, to be called leaders, you must be excellent organizers. Anyway, let's fight bravely together amid the flower-scented breezes of May.

五月　一日

幹部はあくまで礼儀正しく

そして法を説くときは

毅然たる確信ある言動であるべきだ

さらに広布という革命であるならば

見事なる組織者でなければ

幹部とはいえない

ともあれ風薫る五月を

勇敢に戦おう

MAY 2

True victory is only won through courage and tenacity. Leaving fame and vanity behind, let's charge on to blaze trails of glory.

五月二日

真の勝利は
勇気と執念の連続に
よってのみ得られる
見栄をすて
外聞をすてて
体当たりで栄光の道を
切り拓いていこう

MAY 3

Cheerfully
Without fanfare
Without waiting to be told
Even if no one sees our struggle,
Let's each fulfill our own quest and respon-
sibilities as the pioneers of Jiyu.

誰
に
い
わ
れ
な
く
て
も

誰
も
み
て
い
な
く
て
も

地
涌
の
戦
士
は

晴
れ
ば
れ
と
し
て

各
々
の
責
任
と
使
命
を

黙
々
と
果
た
し
き
っ
て
い
こ
う

五
月
三
日

Josei Toda inaugurated second president of Soka Gakkai, 1951.
Daisaku Ikeda inaugurated third president of Soka Gakkai, 1960.

138

MAY 4

Thorough discussion and uncompromising action are the only sources of true friendship and mercy. Let's be aware that these are the actual practice of Buddhism.

徹底した対話と
行動のなかにのみ
真実の友情と慈愛がある
これこそ仏道の実践と
自覚しよう

五月四日

MAY 5

First, give people self-confidence, and all roads will open up from there.

まず自信を
もたせることだ
そこから一切の道が
開かれていくからだ

五月五日

First America Brass Band Recital, 1967.
President Ikeda meets with Dr. Arnold Toynbee, 1972.

MAY 6

Let's work vigorously and lead rich, meaningful lives.

五　月　六　日

逞（たくま）しく働こう
そして豊かな生活を
獲得しよう

MAY 7

Now is the moment to fight boldly, brimming with confidence, in order to turn everything into a rising tide of victory.

五月七日

さあ
自信満々と強気で戦おう
一切を勝利の上げ潮に
かえるために

MAY 8

Never annoy your neighbors by parking
carelessly or through other thoughtless acts.
One inconsiderate action will wipe out a million
beautiful words.

五
月
八
日

駐車などの問題で
絶対に世間に
迷惑をかけてはならない
百万言の講説も
一事の不心得で
反古になる

President Ikeda leaves for France and England, 1973.

MAY 9

Let's read our organization's newspaper thoroughly. That is the driving force of all development.

機関紙を完全に
読みきろう
それが一切の開拓の
原動力となるからだ

五月九日

MAY 10

No matter who he is, everyone definitely has a mission. Let's enable each member to stand up with self-confidence.

五月十日

誰人たりとも
かならず使命があるものだ
全員自信をもって
立ち上がらせていこう

MAY 11

Let's enable everyone to advance, feeling convinced and inspired. To do so, it is vital to be sure and plan with all the members. That is the picture of a true leader.

五月十一日

皆が納得し
張り合いをもって
前進できるようにしよう
それにはかならず
全員にはかることが
大事だ
それが真の指導者の姿だ

MAY 12

Let's have superb teamwork and carry out well-planned campaigns. That is what will drive the wedge for victory.

五月十二日

見事なチームワークをもって
緻密な戦いをしよう
そこにこそ
勝利の深い楔が
打ち込めるからだ

President Ikeda leaves for Australia, India and Sri Lanka, 1964.
First Brass Band, Fife and Drum Corps parade, San Francisco, 1968.

MAY 13

The man who carries out his mission regardless of circumstances will always be the winner in life.

五月十三日

いかなる境遇にあっても
自己の使命を貫く者は
常に人生の
勝利者となろう

President Ikeda leaves for U.S., France, Italy, Switzerland and Holland, 1967.

Jakkozan Honseiji Temple Gohonzon Enshrining Ceremony, President Ikeda and Nittatsu Shonin officiating, 1967.

President Ikeda leaves for France, England and the Soviet Union, 1975.

MAY 14

*Let's do a vibrant Gongyo, work vigor-
ously at our jobs and carry on our activities in
high spirits. Also, let's get to bed early.*

五月十四日

生き生きとした勤行をしよう
生き生きとした仕事をしよう
生き生きとした活動をしよう
夜は早く寝て

MAY 15

Don't make people feel stiff or uncomfortable by being a stickler for formalities. Those with strong faith are flexible about formalities and care more about the heart of things.

五月十五日

形式にこだわって
頑（かたくな）な印象を与えてはいけない
むしろ本質を尊重して
形式には柔軟性をもたせてあげるのが
信心強盛の人のいき方である

MAY 16

Never make unexpected guests feel uncomfortable. Take good care of them so they can go home feeling satisfied. Let's advance, recognizing this as the first step in our activities to promote friendship.

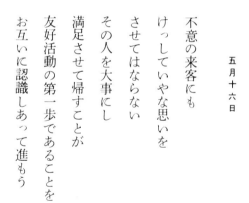

五月十六日

不意の来客にも
けっしていやな思いを
させてはならない
その人を大事にし
満足させて帰すことが
友好活動の第一歩であることを
お互いに認識しあって進もう

President Ikeda establishes America Joint Headquarters, 1967.

Enichizan Myohoji Temple Gohonzon Enshrining Ceremony, President Ikeda and Nittatsu Shonin officiating, 1967.

President Ikeda dedicates Washington D.C. Community Center, 1972.

MAY 17

The benefits of faith blossom through continual effort. Only the efforts that spring from faith can build indestructible fortune.

五月十七日

努力しゆく
その延長のうえに
信心の功徳の花は開き
信心源泉の努力のなかに
初めて確たる
福運は開くのだ

Buddhism is reason, so to act senselessly is to act against Buddhism. From beginning to end, correct faith is found only in day-to-day actions rooted in common sense.

五月十八日

仏法は道理であるゆえに
非常識は謗法である
第一にも第二にも
常識ある生活行動のなかにのみ
正しい信仰はある

New York Community Center Gohonzon Enshrining Ceremony, President Ikeda attending, 1967.

President Ikeda meets with Andre Malraux, 1974.

MAY 19

Leaders should devote themselves wholeheartedly to their members. Take especially good care of older people and learn from their priceless experience.

五月十九日

幹部は
ただひたすらに
会員のために
奉仕することだ
とくに年配者を守り
その大切な経験を
学ぶことだ

President Ikeda opens Malibu Training Center, 1972.

MAY 20

A day when you're out of rhythm will be dark and depressing. To glow with vitality and stay in tune with the highest rhythm all day long, you must do Gongyo and Daimoku without fail.

五月二十日

リズムなき一日は
暗い一日となるがゆえに
明るい活力ある最高の
リズムの日々を送るため
勤行唱題を
断じてなすことだ

MAY 21

*Leaders should talk with all their members
and form strong ties with each of them. These
actions embody the Gohonzon's great im-
partial wisdom (Byodo Daie) and are the
practice of Buddhism.*

幹部はすべからく
会員一人ひとりと対話して
つよく結びあって
いくべきだ
それが平等大慧の行動であり
如来の実践であるからだ

五月二十一日

Los Angeles Convention — Ninth All America General Meeting,
President Ikeda attending, 1972.

MAY 22

We are, you could say, the emmissaries of Buddha. True courage and mercy and the rise of Kosen-rufu are all included in our activities to promote friendship. Be confident on that score, and carry on our movement forever.

五月二十二日

如来の使いの
当体ともいえる私どもの
友好活動のなかには
まさしく勇気も慈愛も
そして広布の拡大も
一切含まれていることを確信して
限りなくこの運動を続けきろう

MAY 23

*Do the job well, and take time to give
thorough guidance. Brick by brick, let's build
our victory.*

五月二十三日

仕事はじっくりかかれ
指導はゆっくり語れ
そして
いつも勝利の建設を
つみ重ねていこう

President Ikeda dedicates America Headquarters Building and Santa
Monica Community Center, 1972.

MAY 24

Above all, let's arise in unity. That is faith. There will be no benefit if we lose the Gakkai spirit.

第一にも第二にも

団結で立ち上がろう

これが信心だ

学会精神を失うところに

功徳はないだろう

五月二十四日

MAY 25

Remember it is the seemingly most ordinary efforts of Gongyo and day-to-day living which encompass world peace, revolution and enlightenment.

五月二十五日

もっとも平凡のような
勤行と生活のなかにこそ
広布も革命も成仏も
含まれていることを
忘れまい

MAY 26

Make friends and be as cheerful as possible in your dealings outside the Gakkai. Mutual understanding is the sublime dialogue of Buddhism, and our contacts with society will pave the way for the spread of the supreme Law (Myoho-rufu).

五月二十六日

できうる限り明朗に
外部と接しよう
親しくなり
互いに疎通することも
堂々たる仏法対話であり
社会的連繋（れんけい）は
妙法流布に通ずるからだ

MAY 27

Bring out your own unique qualities, and enable other people to do the same.

五月二十七日

自己の持味を出せ
そして
人の持味を出さしめよ

MAY 28

Life is long — so is the road to Kosen-rufu. Together, day by day, let's be proud and live to the fullest with hope, self-confidence and generosity.

五月二十八日

ともかく人生も
広布の道も長い
互いに自信と余裕と
希望をいだいて
一日一日を
着実に胸を張って
生きぬくことだ

MAY 29

Live purposefully, day by day. Follow your own road with confidence. Advance steadily on the path you have chosen. That is the true way of Buddhism and the shortest route to personal victory.

五月二十九日

堅実な一日一日を送ろう

わが道を悠々と生きぬこう

わが道を着実に進みゆこう

これこそが

真実の仏法の道であり

その人の勝利の

近道であるからだ

President Ikeda leaves for People's Republic of China, 1974.

MAY 30

Take deliberate, self-assured and cheerful action.

五月三十日

余裕ある行動
自信ある行動
そして
明朗なる行動たれ

MAY 31

Bravely carry out what you feel is worthwhile. That is self-motivated faith. Let's fight again today in high spirits and greatly develop both ourselves and the Gakkai.

五月三十一日

よいと思ったことは
勇気をもって実践しよう
これが主体性ある信心だ
今日も元気にたたかい
自己を　学会を
大きく開いていこう

June

JUNE 1

The prime point of the Gakkai is, and always will be, the people. Never forget that our prayers and exhaustive efforts to protect their happiness will give rise to true human justice.

六月 一日

学会の原点は
あくまでも庶民である
庶民の幸せを守り願う
徹底した行動のなかにこそ
真実の人間正義が
あることを忘れまい

JUNE 2

Practice steadily, like flowing water.
Take calm, well thought-out action.
Give guidance confidently.
And then, have bright, cheerful meetings.

六月二日

水の信心
落ち着いた行動
確信ある指導
そして朗らかな会合

JUNE 3

We embody the supreme Law, so let's take care of ourselves.

The Gohonzon is enshrined in our homes; let's keep them clean.

Then, let's win the trust of the community.

六 月 三 日

妙法の当体たる
わが生命を健康にしよう
御本尊まします
わが家を清潔にしよう
そして地域の人々の
信頼を勝ちとろう

JUNE 4

Gakkai members all share equally the tasks of a general, his staff and troops. All are responsible for Kosen-rufu. Once we awaken to this, we can always achieve great victories.

六月　四日

学会員は
全員が将軍であり
参謀であり兵士であり
広布の責任者である
この陣列の自覚が
常に大勝利を
築いていくのだ

JUNE 5

Win friends and supporters through persistent effort, using every means possible. That is Kosen-rufu.

六　月　五　日

友をつくれ
味方をつくれ
あらゆる方法と
忍耐をもって
それが
広宣流布だ

JUNE 6

No matter how badly we're criticized, let's carry on. We know that glory and victory await us in the course of our persistent struggle.

六月六日

いくらののしられようと
我慢しよう
忍耐の持続のなかにこそ
栄光と勝利が待っていることを
われわれは知っているからだ

First President Tsunesaburo Makiguchi born, 1871.

JUNE 7

Buddhism is strict: win or lose. Your self-awakening at this moment and your resolve to fight courageously will show vivid proof, ten years later. Bear this in mind and have strong faith.

六月七日

仏法の勝負は厳しい
現在の自覚と
勇気ある闘争の決意が
十年後にあまりにも明瞭に
顕われるであろう
心して強き信心たれ

JUNE 8

Let's carry out refreshing activities together, leaving nothing to regret. Let's each win and then sing for joy.

六
月
八
日

お互いに
悔いのない
清々しい活動を
しぬこう
そして各々が
勝って喜び歌おう

JUNE 9

Ultimately the only way to actualize Buddhism is through human revolution. Before criticizing others, you yourself should humbly chant Daimoku and devote yourself to the spread of Buddhism.

ともかく仏法の具体化は

人間革命しかない

人を批判するまえに

謙虚に

まず自分が

唱題と仏法流布に

励んでいくことだ

六月九日

JUNE 10

What is your goal today? Advance steadily in your practice with your targets clear in mind, and all your complaints and onshitsu will vanish.

六月十日

自分の
今日の目標は何か
常に目標を明確にして
前へ進んでいく
実践のなかに
すべての愚痴と怨嫉は
霧散してしまうものだ

JUNE 11

*Let's each become men of faith like iron,
confident that therein lies the world of
enlightenment and the Buddha's land we in-
herently possess (Hon'nu Jakko-do).*

六月十一日

一人ひとりが鉄のごとき
信心の人になろう
そこに仏界があり
本有寂光土なるを確信して

JUNE 12

The more our activities intensify, the more we should chant Daimoku and be sure to get enough sleep to prepare for a successful campaign tomorrow.

活動が活発になればなるほど
豊かなる唱題を重ねて
睡眠を十分にとりながら
悠々たる明日の戦いに
備えよう

六月十二日

JUNE 13

Let's pour our total energy into discussion meetings. All efforts should bear fruit at the discussion meeting; all efforts should begin from the discussion meeting. As leaders, let's seize the initiative with the power of a charging lion. Otherwise there will be no growth and no model of the Gakkai.

六月十三日

座談会に総力をあげよう

一切をそこに結実し

そこより出発すべきだ

獅子奮迅の力をもって

幹部が率先していこう

それ以外に

学会の発展と縮図は断じてない

JUNE 14

No matter how busy you are, never break the rhythm of 'faith equals daily life.' Realize that any action which makes society lose faith in us will obstruct our campaign to broaden our friendships.

六月十四日

どんなに忙しくても
信心即生活のリズムを
けっして狂わせてはならない
社会の信用を失う
すべての行為は
友好拡大の敵と
自覚しよう

JUNE 15

Leaders should each tackle their meetings and conferences in a spirit of total commitment. Let's approach everything constructively and creatively, and consider it from many different angles. That is the bulwark of the Gakkai and the wedge that will open the way to victory.

一切の幹部は
それぞれの会議　会合に
捨て身で取り組もう
すべてを建設的　創造的
多角的に思索して──
それが学会の防壁であり
学会を勝利に導く楔_{くさび}だ

JUNE 16

As the person in charge, put your full effort into conducting each meeting. Be confident that wherever you go, you'll see total victory.

六月十六日

担当者は全力あげて
一切の会合を運営しよう
われ行くところ
完璧な勝利の
実証ありと確信して

JUNE 17

In every campaign, you should carry yourself like a triumphant general, full of high hopes. Since cause and effect are simultaneous (Inga Guji), your Ichinen at this moment is the cause for great victory.

六月十七日

戦いはすべて
凱旋将軍のごとく
満身希望にみちて
振る舞っていこう
大勝利は因果倶時の
一念にあるからだ

JUNE 18

Chant Daimoku sincerely for the people who cause you the most trouble. This too will open up new dimensions in your life, as it is a vital part of the Buddhist practice.

六月十八日

自分の一番困った人のために
題目をあげてあげよう
それもまた
自己の境涯をひろげゆく
大切な仏道修行の
一つだからである

JUNE 19

Since the people we meet are closely linked to us from the eternal past, let's remember to treat others with warmth, sincerity and human kindness.

六月十九日

ともかく
あの人も　この人も
久遠より縁深き人ゆえに
私たちは
誠実と人情味豊かな
接し方を忘れまい

JUNE 20

Since 'Buddhism equals society,' Gakkai members should have a deeper grasp of, and respect for, society. Remember you should be loved and needed by everyone as a leader of people.

六月二十日

仏法即社会であるがゆえに
学会人はもっと社会を熟知し
大切にしながら
あらゆる人から親しまれる
庶民のリーダーであるとの
自覚を忘れまい

JUNE 21

Throughout our campaign, let's protect our fellow members and compensate for each other's shortcomings. Let's forge on in unity, radiant and light-hearted.

戦いには
同志を守り合い
かばいあって前進しよう
お互いにスクラムを組んで
明るく愉しく

六月二十一日

JUNE 22

Wherever you are, become a leader. That way Buddhism will spread naturally in society (Jun'en Kofu).

六月二十二日

自分のおかれた社会の
リーダーになろう
それが順縁広布である

JUNE 23

Let's build sturdy bodies, in keeping with the logic of 'faith equals daily life,' and stride cheerfully and spiritedly in the vanguard of Kosen-rufu.

道理正しい信心即生活で
頑健な身体をつくろう
そして楽しく生き生きと
広布の先陣を歩もう

六月二十三日

JUNE 24

*Be sure to get vital information quickly
and accurately. That is essential to progress.*

六月二十四日

価値ある情報は
正確に迅速に受けよう
それが前進の
重要な要件なれば

JUNE 25

Speak out positively in all situations.
Intelligent, to-the-point comments are golden.
Silence is silver.

いかなる場合でも
積極的に発言すべきである
聡明にして要をえた言々句々は
黄金であり
沈黙は銀である

六月二十五日

JUNE 26

Find capable men.
Protect and foster them.
He who does so
is truly capable.

人材を見つけ出せ
人材を護り育てよう
これをする人が
真の人材なのだ

六月二十六日

JUNE 27

Where unity is strong, there will be victory.
We must never forget this, throughout our lives.

六月二十七日

ともあれ
団結の強いところが
勝つということを
われらは生涯
永遠に忘れまい

JUNE 28

The whole crux of a campaign is to be aggressive. Perfecting a sound strategy and laying thorough groundwork are the secrets of victory.

六月二十八日

戦いの根底はすべて
強気でいかなくてはならぬ
ただし作戦をよく練り
根まわしを充分に
行うことが
勝利の要諦である

JUNE 29

Let's read editorials, in any newspaper.

社説を読もう
いかなる
新聞においても

六月二十九日

JUNE 30

First, let's strengthen our unity like iron.
First, let's practice steadily.
First, let's give guidance with conviction.
Then, undefeated by criticism, let's continue laying strategically solid groundwork for the future.

六月三十日

まず鉄の団結を固めよう
まず地道な実践をしよう
まず確信もって指導にあたろう
そしていかなる批判も
ものともせず
未来への確かな布石を
さらに打っていこう

July

JULY 1

Now it's July and the height of summer.
Challenge this month with all your heart and
spend it as meaningfully as possible.

七月一日

さあ
盛夏の七月を
思う存分戦い
もっとも有意義におくろう

JULY 2

The organization is not a machine. It is life-to-life, human contact. Without such contact we couldn't call this an organization of Wagoso. Leaders must bear this in mind and continually inspire pure faith.

七月二日

組織は機械ではない
生命と生命の
ふれ合いである
それがなければ
和合僧の組織とはいえない
幹部は心して
清浄な信心の源泉となれ

JULY 3

Remember that he who upholds his conviction to practice exactly as Buddhism teaches (Nyosetsu Shugyo) is the one who will be praised by Nichiren Daishonin.

七月三日

ともあれ
如説修行の信念の持続の人こそ
日蓮大聖人より
称賛される人と
自覚することだ

Second President Toda released from Toyotama Prison, 1945.

JULY 4

Develop your personal guidance and encouragement, and deepen your individual relationships. That is the cause for all victories.

七
月
四
日

個人の指導　激励を深め
個人との
結合を深くせよ
これ一切の
勝利の因なれば

Denver Convention, 1970.

JULY 5

The man of vanity who (out of love for his own ego and the limelight) scorns the noble effort behind the scenes, will, at the close of his life, find only emptiness.

七　月　五　日

自身のエゴと売名のため
尊い陰の労作業を
嘲(ちょうしょう)笑する虚栄の人は
人生の最後は
虚無感しか
残らないであろう

JULY 6

Be strict with yourself.
Be generous with others.
Then, work to harmonize the whole.

自己には厳しく
人には寛大に
そして
全体の調和をはかろう

七月六日

JULY 7

Be aware that your own progress comes through persevering in your practice, day by day, with hope and self-confidence.

自己の向上は
希望ある日々と
自信をもった忍耐の
実践からと知れ

七月七日

JULY 8

Let's go to bed early and get up early. That is the basis for sound progress and development.

七　月　八　日

早くやすもう
そして早く起きよう
そこにこそ逞しい前進と
建設があるからだ

JULY 9

Those in charge must be brimming with youthful confidence and make all the members feel convinced and delighted. A general of Myoho must master the study of inspiring others.

七月九日

すべての担当者は
若々しく確信に満ちみち
全員が納得し
歓喜するように
せねばならぬ
それが妙法の
将軍学である

JULY 10

Let's read our organization's newspaper and magazine thoroughly. Neglecting these publications means neglecting Kosen-rufu. Reading them, however, is the driving force of faith, or in other words, means protecting the unity of our organization (Wagoso) and the Dai-Gohonzon.

七月十日

機関紙・誌を熟読しよう
機関紙・誌を軽視することは
広宣流布を軽視することに
通ずるからだ
機関紙・誌を読むことは
信心の前進を推進し　即　和合僧を守り
大御本尊を守ることに通ずるからだ

JULY 11

My fellow members! Let's advance, proudly affirming the sublime, outstanding proof of Kosen-rufu which the Soka Gakkai has achieved thus far.

叫び進もう
誉れ高く
広宣流布の実証を
偉大なる
崇高にして
創価学会のこれまでの
わが同志よ

七月十一日

Young Men's Division established, 1951.

JULY 12

Let's still further improve our discussion meetings. Bringing our friends and enabling our fellow members to stand up and participate will result in great benefit. These actions may be called the ideal faith for our times.

七月十二日

座談会をさらに盛り上げよう

そこに友人を伴ってくることも

同志を立ち上がらせて

参加させることも

偉大な功徳である

この実践こそ

完全なる時の信心といえよう

JULY 13

"I chant, so I don't have to worry"—this is carelessness, not the true spirit of 'faith equals daily life.' Remember that he who pays strict attention to reality and leads a life free from accident has real faith and will be protected by the Shoten Zenjin.

七月十三日

信心があるがゆえに
安心であるという油断は
真の信心即生活ではない
現実に厳しく注意し
無事の人生　生活をしていくところに
真の信心があるといえよう
そこに諸天の加護が
あることを忘れまい

JULY 14

A merging of cheerfulness, courtesy and sincerity is an expression of faith. Remember that Kosen-rufu will unfold through such actions.

七月十四日

明朗と礼儀と誠実の結晶が
信心の発露であるがゆえに
その人の行動があるところに
広布は展開されていくことを
忘れまい

JULY 15

The long march to Kosen-rufu demands a sound body, an unyielding spirit. This summer, together, let's train ourselves rigorously.

遠い広宣流布の
転教の行進には
頑強なる色心が
要求されるゆえに
この夏は共々に
大いに生命を鍛錬しよう

七月十五日

JULY 16

In the Gakkai, embodying justice and courageous practice, there is nothing we have to fear, for we are confident of the power of our faith whose lifeblood flows directly from Nichiren Daishonin.

七月十六日

わが正義と
実践の学会には
なにも恐れるものはない
日蓮大聖哲と直結の
脈々とした信心の強さを
確信しているからだ

Nichiren Daishonin submits *Rissho Ankoku Ron* to Hojo Regency, 1260.

JULY 17

*Never forget that only one-to-one guid-
ance and dialogue will give rise to productive
action embodying the true prime point.*

七月十七日

一対一の指導
一対一の対話
そこにのみ空転のない
真実の原点行動があることを
絶対に忘れてはならない

JULY 18

Today, rather than leading a seemingly pleasurable life of self-indulgence, you should toil, bathed in sweat, on the road of the Buddhist practice, so that tomorrow you can live a life filled with confidence.

七月十八日

今日　放縦で幸せそうに

みえる人生になるよりも

明日　確信に満ちみちた

人生をおくれる人になるために

今日も汗を流し

仏法実践の軌跡に

生きることだ

JULY 19

The campaign is not waged in the distance,
nor does your happiness lie far from you.
Awaken to why you are where you are, and
resolutely defend your battle stations.

戦いは遠くに
あるものではない
幸福も遠くに
あるものではない
自分自身が
その地域にあることを自覚して
各部署を守り抜くことだ

七月十九日

Young Women's Division established, 1951.
First All America Women's Division Meeting, Los Angeles, 1967.

JULY 20

No matter how valid a man's statements may sound, if he's not practicing as the True Buddha teaches (Nyosetsu Shugyo), he is irresponsible and, in effect, acting against Buddhism. You should have a sharp eye for this.

七月二十日

いくら正論を
吐いたように思えても
如説修行の軌跡なきは
所詮　懈怠謗法であることを
鋭く見抜くことだ

JULY 21

*Now that the time is ripe for our move-
ment, forcing our beliefs on others or acting in
ways which offend people is nothing short of
stupidity. Let's be flexible always and conduct
our activities in style.*

七月二十一日

機　熟している

この時代にあって

信仰のことで無理じいしたり

嫌悪されるような行動は
けんお

もはや愚かといわざるをえない

ともかく柔軟な姿勢で

スマートに活躍しよう

JULY 22

*Let's protect our districts no matter what.
Let's build and develop them. Therein lies the
whole campaign of Kosen-rufu.*

わが大ブロックを

断じて守ろう

築こう

拓こう

ここにこそ

広宣流布の法戦の

一切があるからだ

七月二十二日

JULY 23

Today may be hard — the ascent cruelly steep — but we are sons of the Gakkai. Once again, let's join in strong unity and courageously march on to the fresh, green fields that await us.

七月二十三日

今日が辛（つら）くても

　そして

今　険難な山でも

われら学会っ子は

スクラムを固く組みなおして

次の緑滴（したた）る曠野まで

勇敢に前に進もう

JULY 24

The summer course has started! My friends, whether you can attend or not, enjoy your study of the ultimate life-philosophy of our day, but tackle it also as a meaningful challenge to train yourselves and contribute to society.

七月二十四日

さあ　夏季講習会だ
現代最高峰の生命哲理を
楽しみつつ
有意義に取り組もう
自らの錬磨のため
社会への貢献のため
参加する友もできぬ友も

Ikeda Ocean View Gardens Opening Ceremony at Pupukea, President Ikeda attending, 1975.

JULY 25

Steady faith, consistent action and a secure, balanced life — this is the posture most befitting Gakkai members today. Remember once you adopt it, even those who normally waver will feel reassured and come seeking you.

七月二十五日

安定した信仰
安定した行動
安定した生活

これこそ現時点での最も正しい

学会人の姿勢とせねばならない

そこに初めて

心の動揺に終始する人々も

安心して求めてくることを忘れまい

Seattle Convention — Eighth All America General Meeting, 1971.

JULY 26

*Let's strive still harder to perfect our lives,
our jobs and our organization, while at the
same time, creating new trends.*

自己の生活と職場を
またわが組織を
さらに完備していこう
新しい潮流を
つくりながら

七月二十六日

Washington D.C. Convention in Santa Monica — Sixth All America
General Meeting, Los Angeles, 1969.

Hawaii Pre-Bicentennial Convention — Twelfth NSA General Meeting
held in Honolulu, President Ikeda attending, 1975.

JULY 27

Before you theorize, practice. Theory is for the sake of practice. Through the practice of Ichinen Sanzen you can open up vast, new realms.

われらは論ずるより
まず実践だ
論ずることは
実践のためにある
この一念三千の
実践によってこそ
新たなる偉大な
開拓がなされるのだ

JULY 28

Only confident guidance and confident
action will give rise to immense benefit.

確信の指導
確信の行動
そこにのみ
大功徳は湧く

七月二十八日

JULY 29

Let's each resolve to grow tremendously and complete another stage of construction together during July and August, with the traditional summer training course as our foundation.

七月二十九日

ともどもに七月八月は

伝統の講習会を軸に

一人ひとりが

大きな成長　建設の

節と決めよう

JULY 30

Let's stand up with the spirit of Abutsubo and dedicate ourselves to a practice linked directly with the Dai-Gohonzon. That is the source of real faith and real joy.

七月三十日

すべての人が
阿仏房の精神に立って
大御本尊に直結した
信心に励もう
そこに真の信心と
歓喜があるのだ

JULY 31

Be confident that the present decides the future (Gento Nise), that results are born in the same instant the cause is made (Inga Guji), and wherever you are, drive home a wedge for progress. That is the real faith of 'now is my last moment.'

その場所その場所で
完璧な楔を打ちこもう
"現当二世" と "因果倶時" を確信して
これが "只今臨終" の
真実の信心であるからだ

August

AUGUST 1

The character 'eight' means to open.
Throughout August, the eighth month, let's
chant clear, resonant Daimoku and accomplish
a full year's growth.

八月一日

八とは開く義なり
八月を一年間の
大成長の節にしよう
題目を朗々とあげきって

AUGUST 2

*Remember the world of Kosen-rufu is
found nowhere else but in the blossoming of a
single family, or in society's trust for a single
individual.*

八月二日

一人の人間の
社会からの信頼と
花咲く一家の
姿のなかにのみ
広布の世界が
あることを忘れまい

AUGUST 3

*Let's take the very best care of those
people who bring guests to discussion meetings,
as it will generate a fresh wave of change.
Leaders should give this their close attention.*

学会の会合に
誘い連れてくる人を
もっとも大切にすることが
革新の波動になることを
幹部は心していかねばならない

八月 三日

AUGUST 4

Remember that people only feel at ease and gather around a leader with a warm smile and unwavering confidence in faith.

八月　四日

あたたかい笑顔と
強靱なる信仰の確信を
たもちゆく指導者のなかにのみ
人々は安心して
集い来ることを
忘れまい

AUGUST 5

Only those who make consistent efforts in Daimoku, study and neighborhood discussion meetings are true and honorable Gakkai members. That is the standard I would like to set.

八月五日

ともかく題目と教学と
地域の座談会の活動を
持続していく人のみが
真(まこと)の誉(ほま)れある
学会員であることを
基準としたいものである

AUGUST 6

Those strong in faith at a crucial moment are sure to be winners in life. Undeterred by whatever storms arise, let's advance with the fresh breeze of autumn to open new roads.

八月六日

大事な時に強靱な信仰の人は
かならず人生の勝利者となる
われらはいかなる風波にも動ぜず
秋風と共に爽やかに
新しい道を開き進むことだ

AUGUST 7

'*He who is strong when he stands alone is truly brave.*' With this as our watchword, let's fight gallantly and pioneer new ground in every field of endeavor. Read the Gosho little by little and live each day courageously.

八月七日

〝一人立てる時に強き者は
真正の勇者なり〟を合い言葉に
あらゆる分野で堂々と戦い
道を拓こう
ともかく御書を少しずつ読み
勇気ある一日一日を
過ごすことだ

AUGUST 8

Traditionally this is now the summer
month of guidance. During a time which so
many people spend in leisure, let's increase our
fortune by enjoying our practice.

八月八日

さあ
伝統の夏季指導の月だ
人がレジャーですごすとき
われらはより以上の
楽しい福運をつみゆこう

AUGUST 9

Let's get rid of onshitsu, as it cuts off the source of benefit. Above all, let's advance in unity and solidify the stronghold of discussion meetings. This is the faith that befits our times.

八月九日

怨嫉はやめよう

功徳の根を断ち切るからだ

第一にも第二にも

団結で進もう

そして座談会の牙城を

完璧に構築しよう

これが時の信心だ

AUGUST 10

Armed with unshakeable conviction, let's train ourselves this August in both body and spirit, so we can get a head start and win and prosper in everything.

八月十日

さあ
われらが八月を
逞しい信念で
色心ともに鍛えよう
すべての勝利と
繁栄のために
機先を制するために

AUGUST 11

Don't be swept along by force of habit.
Take the initiative in each campaign.

惰性に流されるな
すべての戦いに
先手をうて

八月十一日

First America-Europe Joint Leaders' Meeting opens in Paris, 1966.
President Ikeda leaves for the United States, 1973.

AUGUST 12

Let's be strict about getting to meetings on time. Those in charge especially must not be late. That is the way of a true leader.

八月十二日

お互いに会合の時間を
厳守しよう
とくに担当者は
遅刻せぬこと
それが
真の指導者だ

AUGUST 13

Sleep well and have continually fresh and vigorous activities.

八月十三日

よく寝て
いつも生き生きした
活動を

Fourth All America General Meeting, San Francisco, 1967.

244

AUGUST 14

Let's protect our community centers, the castles of the Law for the eternal prosperity of true Buddhism. This will mean progress toward a new era.

正法久住の法城である
本部会館を大切にしよう
それが新時代の前進だ

八月十四日

President Ikeda leaves for U.S., 1965.
Third All America General Meeting, New York, 1966.
President Ikeda opens Maui Community Center, 1973.

AUGUST 15

A man drunk on his past achievements is backsliding. Leaders must always live for the future.

昨日までの
功績に酔う者は
退歩と知れ
指導者は常に
未来に生きよ

八月十五日

World Tribune publishes first issue, 1964.

Enichizan Myohoji Temple Groundbreaking Ceremony, President Ikeda attending, 1965.

AUGUST 16

Be warm toward those working behind the scenes and speak courteously to your juniors, no matter who they are.

八月十六日

陰の人にあたたかく
そして後輩には
誰人たりとも
丁寧な言葉遣いを

AUGUST 17

*Let's keep track of our household accounts
and turn our lifestyles into prosperous ones.*

家計簿をつけよう
そして生活設計を
裕福に転換させていこう

八月十七日

AUGUST 18

*Do a beautiful Gongyo, morning and
evening. That is the source of all actual proof.*

五座三座の勤行を
立派にやることだ
そこにこそ真実の
一切の実証はあろう

八月十八日

Pan-American Nichiren Shoshu League founded, 1973.

AUGUST 19

Have confidence in yourself. Have hopes and conviction. That takes consistent Daimoku, since only Daimoku encompasses all human activity.

八月十九日

自信をもて
希望をもて
確信をもて
それには題目を
唱えきることだ
そこにのみ
一切の人生の活動が
含まれるからだ

AUGUST 20

No matter what anyone says, you should report the facts just as they are. This will be a source of great strength and create opportunities for self-reflection. It also shows the real meaning of 'faith equals all phenomena.'

八月二十日

あらゆる連絡　報告は
ありのままの事実で
あるべきだ
それが最大の強みであり
反省であり
真実の信心即一切法である
だれになんといわれようと

Jakkozan Honseiji Temple opens in Honolulu, President Ikeda attending, 1966.

Scolding is not necessarily guidance. Guidance means making people understand. Instructions and orders are not guidance, either. Leading others through the power of actual proof is guidance.

叱_{しか}ることが指導ではない

納得させることが指導だ

また命令　指示が指導ではなく

事実の力で引導することが

指導である

AUGUST 22

Exert your full effort in giving individual guidance. That is the core of great development. All efforts will be fruitless where one-to-one guidance has been neglected.

個人指導に全力をあげよう
それが大なる発展の
核になるのだ
個々の指導を
避けたところは
すべて空転してしまうからだ

八月二十二日

AUGUST 23

Put an end to onshitsu. It is your enemy and stands in the way of benefit. Let's enable everyone to fulfill all their desires with fresh, honest faith linked directly to the Dai-Gohonzon.

八月二十三日

怨嫉は絶対やめよう

功徳をふさぐ

自身の敵であるからだ

大御本尊と直結した

若々しい素直な信心で

皆を所願満足させよう

AUGUST 24

The whole of Buddhism exists within society. Those ignorant of the ways of the world are not really practicing Buddhism. Be strict with yourself. You must live, win and prosper in society — that is the real meaning of 'Buddhism equals society.'

八月二十四日

仏法はすべて社会のなかにある

世間知らずは

仏法の真の実践者とはいえない

心して社会に生き

社会に勝ち　社会に厳しく

そして社会に栄えていかねばならぬ

それが仏法即社会だ

President Ikeda joins Nichiren Shoshu Soka Gakkai, 1947.

AUGUST 25

*Let's read our organization's newspaper
and have other people read it too, realizing that
it gives us the energy to take action.*

機関紙を読もう
そして読ませよう
われらの行動の
エネルギーと自覚して

八月二十五日

First All America General Meeting, Chicago, 1963.

Hawaii Convention — Fifth All America General Meeting, Honolulu, 1968.

AUGUST 26

Now is the time to unite and once again advance boldly and cheerfully to open new worlds.

さあ
再びスクラムを組んで
新天地の開拓に逞しく
朗らかに前進しよう

八月二十六日

AUGUST 27

Never be stupidly optimistic or take society's affairs too lightly. The Gosho states, 'It is a wonder when things go well. It is a matter of course that things go badly.' You should assume leadership with this firmly in your mind; otherwise, there can be no campaign of Myoho.

八月二十七日

物事を　社会を
絶対に甘く考えてはならぬ
「よからんは不思議
悪しからんは一定」の御聖訓を
身に刻んで指揮をとるべきだ
それ以外に妙法の闘争はない

AUGUST 28

Protect your own sphere of activity. Win and be trusted there. That is the true picture of 'enlightenment equals the nine worlds.'

それぞれの社会を
大切にしよう
その社会で信頼され
勝つことだ
これが仏界即九界の
実相である

八月二十八日

AUGUST 29

You cannot spread Buddhism by exhorting others. Leaders must be the first to practice. He who carries out activities himself and also motivates others to practice deserves to be called a great general.

八月二十九日

仏法拡大は掛け声ではなくして
まず幹部から実践することだ
自ら活動し
人をも実践活動に
いたらしめてこそ
名将というべきである

AUGUST 30

Keep your daily life fresh and abreast of the times. This is faith, and the road to swift progress. A weary existence means you are defeated.

日々斬新的な
生命を保つことだ
これが信心であり
躍進への道となる
疲れた生命は
自己の敗北を
意味するからだ

八月三十日

AUGUST 31

*Let's find capable men. Let's raise and
protect them. That is the wellspring of eternal
prosperity.*

人材を見つけよう
人材を守ろう
人材を育てよう
それが永遠に栄えゆく源泉だ

八月三十一日

September

SEPTEMBER 1

*September's here — a time for reading.
Let's study the Gosho and read our
organization's newspaper thoroughly. Let's
also tackle worthwhile books and make them
part of our lives.*

九月一日

さあ　読書の九月だ
御書を拝読しよう
機関紙を読みきろう
そして　われわれの
血肉となる指導書を
思いきり読もう

SEPTEMBER 2

Become an expert in your own field. That is actual proof of faith. He who keeps striving diligently at his work is sure to be a winner in the end.

九
月
二
日

その道の
エキスパートになることだ
それが信心の実証である
自己の仕事にあって
勉強しぬく人こそ
かならず最後に勝利者となろう

SEPTEMBER 3

The crisp days of autumn have arrived.
Once again, let's dance for joy on the stage of
our next glorious campaign, singing the highest
praise of the life we are leading.

九月　三日

さあ　爽快な秋だ
再び次の栄えある舞台に
勇躍踊り出でよう
わが人生を最高に
謳歌しながら

SEPTEMBER 4

Whatever the subject, explain it kindly until the other person fully understands. Remember this point in enabling him to give full play to his capabilities.

どんなことでも相手が
十分納得のいくまで
親切に教えてあげよう
それが相手に力を
発揮させるポイントで
あることを忘れまい

九月四日

SEPTEMBER 5

The long road of Kosen-rufu lies ahead of us, so we should remember to wind up our daily Gakkai activities on time. Let's stick to the basic rule of ending all meetings by 9:30.

九 月 五 日

長い広布の旅路であるがゆえに

日々の学会活動では

時間の区切りを

忘れてはならない

ともかく一切の会合は

九時半には終える原則を

厳守しよう

SEPTEMBER 6

In any undertaking, you should seize the
initiative, persevere and have self-confidence.

なんでも先手を打て
なんでも粘りでゆけ
なんでも自信をもつことだ

九月六日

SEPTEMBER 7

Let's let a fresh breeze sweep through our discussion meetings, and be sure to inject something that will satisfy those who attend. Leaders of the four divisions should pool their ingenuity with everyone else and think up all kinds of ways to make this happen.

九月七日

座談会には
新風を吹き込み
出席者が満足するなにかを
かならず注入しよう
四者の中心者をはじめ
皆があらゆる工夫をして

SEPTEMBER 8

*'Faith equals practice,' therefore, it is faith
expressed through action that is in accord with
the Buddha's will. The actions of Gakkai
activities are the true Buddhist practice and will
lead to the flowering of great benefit.*

九月八日

信心は即実行にある
ゆえに信心が行動に現れてこそ
仏意にかなうのだ
学会活動という行動のなかに
真の仏道修行があり
大功徳の花が咲こう

President Ikeda leaves for Soviet Union, 1974.

SEPTEMBER 9

Do Gongyo faithfully each day and read the Gosho little by little. Let's grow and polish ourselves during the meaningful month of September.

九月九日

日々の勤行を
確実にやろう
御書を少しずつでも読もう
そして
この意義ある九月
自分を磨き成長させよう

SEPTEMBER 10

Leaders should always strive for successful discussion meetings. It is also vital to talk with people individually, give them self-confidence and guide them toward happiness.

九月十日

幹部は常に
充実した座談会を
推進しよう
そして
一人ひとりと話し合い
自信をあたえ
幸せに導くことが大事だ

SEPTEMBER 11

Those in charge should be strict about starting meetings on time. Otherwise you will cause people trouble. Such a lack of consideration will destroy us from within, as it creates a cause for failure.

決まった会合時間
担当は厳守せよ
それを破って
民衆に迷惑をかけることは
師子身中の虫だ
敗北の因をつくるからだ

SEPTEMBER 12

Bravely dash to the vanguard of Kosen-
rufu. Hurl yourselves into the battle and reach
one person after another. Only this strict way of
practice leads to victory in all campaigns.

九月十二日

広布の最先端に
勇敢に飛び込もう
そして一人ひとりに
体当たりしよう
その厳しい実践のみが
即すべての勝利に
通じるのだ

Tatsunokuchi Persecution, 1271.

SEPTEMBER 13

Challenge everything as though in hand-to-hand combat. We should be especially thorough in giving guidance, as superficial guidance only confuses people.

九月十三日

すべて一対一の
肉弾戦でいこう
とくに指導は
完璧_{かんぺき}になさねばならぬ
安直な指導はかえって
人を惑わすからだ

SEPTEMBER 14

Let's pour our full effort into each discussion meeting. Bringing people together for a meeting and then making it a success is a victory for Kosen-rufu. It is also great Shakubuku and the practice which befits our times.

九月十四日

おのおの座談会に
総力をあげよう
座談会に結集させ
成功させていくことが
広布への勝利であり
大折伏である
これが時に適った信心である

SEPTEMBER 15

Let's protect sincere members and watch out for the smallest details of their welfare. Let's help them both in faith and in worldly affairs.

九月十五日

よき学会人を
きめ細かに見守り
応援しよう
信心のうえでも
社会のうえでも

First, chant Daimoku.
First, be in good health.
First, work cheerfully.
First, establish your finances.
And first, take the initiative.

まず題目をあげよう
まず身体を健康にしよう
まず元気に働こう
まず経済を確立しよう
そしてまず
率先して動こう

九月十六日

SEPTEMBER 17

Get up early in the morning and do Gongyo. Fight productively and be full of enthusiasm in the evening, and get to bed earlier.

九月十七日

朝は早く起き
五座の勤行を
夜は情熱あふれ
価値的に戦い
早目に休養を

SEPTEMBER 18

Never cause stupid accidents. Act with common sense.

けっして愚かな
事故を起こすな
常識豊かな
行動たれ

九月十八日

Men's Division Inaugural Meeting, Los Angeles, 1966.

SEPTEMBER 19

Win people's trust in everything. That is both your own victory and a victory for Kosen-rufu.

すべてに
信用をつむことだ
それが自己の
勝利であり
広布の勝利と知れ

九月十九日

SEPTEMBER 20

Never cause trouble for your neighbors.
The foundations of Kosen-rufu can't be com-
pleted till you win them over.

九月二十日

隣近所に絶対
迷惑をかけるな
隣近所を味方にした時に
はじめて広宣流布の
完璧な基盤が
出来上がるのだ

SEPTEMBER 21

In home visitation, the leader should personally take time to talk with each member of the family. Only then can you develop each individual's happiness.

家庭指導は
幹部自ら一人ひとりと
じっくり懇談することだ
そこに初めて
個人の幸福が
築かれていく

SEPTEMBER 22

Detailed communication is the first step of the campaign. That is the practice of Itai Doshin which will save people from unhappiness and protect the Gakkai.

戦いはまず

連絡を密にすることだ

それが人を救い

学会を守りゆく

異体同心の実践である

九月二十二日

SEPTEMBER 23

Stand alone. Never be swept along by force of habit. Build a solid core in each individual.

一人立て
けっして惰性に流されるな
一人ひとりの核を
つくりきれ

九月二十三日

SEPTEMBER 24

Guidance is not merely encouragement.
Guidance begins with mercy (Jihi) and enables
another person to gain absolute confidence.

九月二十四日

指導とは
たんなる激励ではない
指導とは慈悲より出発し
人をして絶対なる確信を
得せしめることだ

SEPTEMBER 25

*The long-awaited fall season is here at last.
Let's read, write and be sure to take a step
forward in everything.*

九月二十五日

さあ　待望の秋だ
読み書き
そしてすべてに
かならず一歩前進しよう

SEPTEMBER 26

Let's take pains to raise each of our members to be individuals of great faith, without a single exception.

九月二十六日

わが同志の
個人個人を
じっくりと大信者に
育てよう
一人も残らずに

SEPTEMBER 27

Be calm and self-assured in both your actions and guidance. Remember no other kind of conduct or influence can continue to light the hearts of the people.

落ち着いて行動し
落ち着いて指導する
行為と響きのなかにのみ
庶民の心の奥に
光をとどめゆけることを
忘れまい

SEPTEMBER 28

Listen carefully to what each person has to say. Then give guidance with a tone of justice and fairness which will remain in their hearts.

あの人の話も聞いてあげよう

この人の話も聞いてあげよう

そして最後には

正義の論調を

その人の心にとどめゆけるような

指導を忘れまい

SEPTEMBER 29

Let's develop our world boldly through our own efforts, striving to be best in the nation in all we do.

われらの世界を
われらで逞（たくま）しく
築いていこう
そしてすべてに
日本一を目指して

九月二十九日

SEPTEMBER 30

*Let's protect the Gakkai, build the Gakkai
and make the Gakkai prosper. My dear friends:
once again, let's rise heroically in this cause.*

学会を守れ

学会を築け

学会を栄えさせよう

そのために同志よ

再び立ち上がろう

雄々しく

九月三十日

October

OCTOBER 1

*The fall month of October has arrived.
Let's you and I, in perfect teamwork, initiate
fresh progress.*

十月一日

さあ
秋の十月だ
完璧なチームワークで
すがすがしい前進を
開始しよう
君も僕も
あなたも私も

President Toda issues *Youth, Be Patriotic*, 1954.

OCTOBER 2

*He whose words are sought after, whose
actions are trusted and whose attitude is one of
tolerance and understanding can win great
support and develop capable people.*

十月二日

慕われる言語
信頼される行動
すべてを包容する態度
この実相が
多くの味方をつくり
人材をつくるのだ

President Ikeda leaves on first trip abroad, to U.S., Canada and Brazil,
1960.

President Ikeda leaves for Italy, France, Czechoslovakia, Hungary and
Turkey, 1964.

OCTOBER 3

Leaders should not baby themselves. Be strict in developing your own faith and guts, and the Gohonzon will never fail to protect you.

十月三日

幹部は甘えるな
自身の信心と根性で
厳しく成長することだ
さればかならず
御本尊に見守られるであろう

OCTOBER 4

*Communicate and report promptly. That
is the crossroads of victory or defeat.*

連絡　報告を
迅速にせよ
これ勝敗の岐路なれば

十
月
四
日

President Ikeda leaves for Denmark, West Germany, Holland, France,
England, Spain, Switzerland and Austria, 1961.

OCTOBER 5

Develop a strong, healthy body. To that end, you should sleep well, live dynamically each day and devote yourself to the practice of 'faith equals daily life.'

十月五日

ともかく
身体を頑健にしよう
そのためには
よく睡眠をとって
日々の生きいきとした
信仰即生活に
励みゆくことだ

President Ikeda vows world Kosen-rufu atop Telegraph Hill, San Francisco, 1960.

OCTOBER 6

Remember that sincere and courteous words express your own humanity and show the highest regard for the other person as an individual.

十月六日

丁重な　誠実な
言葉遣いこそ
自らの人間性の表れであり
相手の人格を
もっとも尊重する
姿勢であることを
忘れまい

Before worrying or doubting, a man of true faith will carry out the practice of Gongyo. Remember that is the road to and root of all solutions.

十月七日

まことの信仰者ならば
悩むまえに
疑うまえに
まず勤行を実践することだ
そこにこそ
一切の解決の道と
根本があることを忘れまい

Dai-Gohonzon transferred from Hoanden to Sho-Hondo, 1972.

OCTOBER 8

If we are true sons of the Gakkai, let us ride forth, armed with justice, courage and action, into every field of human endeavor.

真の学会っ子なれば
正義と勇気と
行動とをもって
すべての分野で
打って出よう

十月八日

OCTOBER 9

Having strong faith and driving yourself beyond reason are entirely different things. You can overtax yourself only so long; it may look sincere, but you can't keep it up. Strong faith means to be resolute and make steady progress, while maintaining the spark of your own identity.

十月九日

無理と強信とはまったく違う
無理とは一時（いっとき）は
真剣に見えたとしても
長続きしない
強信は遅（たくま）しさと
発現を点滅させながら
常に進歩　持続の
姿勢があるからだ

OCTOBER 10

Win all debates, no matter what. Conviction and courage are the basis of victory. Cowardice is an enemy of Buddhism, for it is the cause of your own unhappiness.

十月十日

あらゆる理論闘争に

断じて勝て

その根本は

確信と勇気である

臆病（おくびょう）は仏法の敵であり

自己の不幸の因で

あるからだ

OCTOBER 11

Welcome and adopt good suggestions.
This is our first step in raising capable people.

十月十一日

いい意見はどしどし聞き
採用することだ
これが互いの
人材育成の
第一歩になるのである

Sho-Hondo Convention — 10th NSA General Meeting and Impossible
Dream Show held at Daisekiji, President Ikeda attending, 1973.

OCTOBER 12

When we've made allies even of all demons and devils, that is Kosen-rufu, for the road to our goal will open and our progress accelerate in the course of that battle.

いかなる悪鬼魔神でも
味方にできたときが
広宣流布である
その戦いのなかにこそ
広布への道が
加速度をもって
開けていくからだ

十月十二日

Dai-Gohonzon inscribed, 1279.
Invocation Ceremony for Sho-Hondo Construction, 1967.
Sho-Hondo Completion Ceremony, 1972.

Let's develop sound, healthy bodies by any means possible. As long as one individual fails to perfect himself, Kosen-rufu cannot be perfected either.

あらゆる方法で
お互いに身体を頑健にしよう
一個の生命の完成なくして
広布の完成は
ありえない

十月十三日

Nichiren Daishonin dies, 1282.

OCTOBER 14

Those irresponsible in their daily lives—especially in regard to money—are never individuals of strong faith. Bear this in mind and uphold the principle of 'faith equals daily life.'

生活なかんずく
金銭にみだらな人に
強信者は一人もいない
心して信心即生活を
打ちたてることだ

十月十四日

OCTOBER 15

Let's fight. Let's work. Let's advance. We are carrying out the practice of Buddhism. Once you awaken to this your complaints will vanish, and everything will open up for you like a starry sky.

十月十五日

戦おう　働こう　進もう

われらは仏道修行をしているのだ

この一点にめざめた時は

愚痴<ruby>愚痴<rt>ぐち</rt></ruby>などは出ぬはずである

その人には一切が

満目<ruby>満目<rt>まんもく</rt></ruby>の星天<ruby>星天<rt>ほしぞら</rt></ruby>と開けよう

OCTOBER 16

Make your own unique skills and qualities first-rate. That is revealing your true and highest potential (Jitai Kensho) for Kosen-rufu.

十月十六日

自己の特技
特色を一流とせよ
これが広宣流布への
自体顕照だ

OCTOBER 17

Don't lose the spirit, 'I've got to win.'
Remember, 'Never relax in the moment of
victory.' Once again, let's courageously forge
on.

十月十七日

"成せばなる" の精神
"勝って兜の緒をしめよ" の精神
これを忘れずに
再び勇ましく
前進を開始しよう

OCTOBER 18

Let's attend discussion meetings. Let's invite others. Together, let's create a splendid battleground of the supreme Law.

十月十八日

座談会に出よう
誘おう
そして見事な法戦場を
皆で創りあげよう

OCTOBER 19

*Always be open to good suggestions,
whether from your juniors or from your seniors.*

良い意見は
どしどしとり入れよ
上下の関係なく

十月十九日

President Ikeda leaves for France, West Germany, Italy and Portugal,
1965.

OCTOBER 20

Develop and train yourself
before criticizing others.

まず自分をつくれ

自分を養え

人々の批判をする前に

十月二十日

OCTOBER 21

Go home early at night, chant Daimoku and build up your spirits. Start out fresh in the morning with powerful vitality.

十月二十一日

夜は早く帰り
題目を唱え
鋭気を養おう
朝は逞しき生命力で
若々しく出発しよう

OCTOBER 22

A man who dozes off in the daytime is a straggler in life.

昼間
居眠りをするような人は
人生の敗残兵と知れ

十月二十二日

President Ikeda establishes America General Chapter, 1960.

OCTOBER 23

Leaders should not spin their wheels. Drive wedges day by day and make sure to keep everything running in gear.

十月二十三日

指導者は空回りするな
日々楔を打て
一切がギアに
はまるように
心して動くべきだ

OCTOBER 24

People are creatures of feeling. Take the utmost care in how you speak to others, regardless of your relative status or position. We should also gladly encourage each other, as there is no other way to build the unity of Itai Doshin.

人は感情の動物である

言葉遣いに上下の別なく

最善の注意を払おう

そしてお互いに

気持ちよく励まし合っていこう

そこにのみ異体同心の

団結が築かれるからだ

十月二十四日

OCTOBER 25

Now is the time to charge ahead: in spreading Buddhism, in guidance and in discussion meetings.

十月二十五日

さあ
体当たりでいこう
仏法拡大に
指導に
会合に

OCTOBER 26

*Remember when you feel you're in love
with the Gohonzon and can't wait to do
Gongyo each day, life will be unspeakably
happy and your efforts will bear fruit without
fail.*

勤行が好きでたまらない

御本尊が好きでたまらない

という日々のところに

人生は楽しくてたまらない

自得の結果が生まれゆくことを

確認しよう

十月二十六日

First Student Division General Meeting, UCLA, 1969.

OCTOBER 27

Take strict precautions against traffic acci-dents, fires and other mishaps. Remember this is the foundation of 'faith equals daily life.'

十月二十七日

交通事故や火災など
事故を未然に防ぐ
細心の厳しき注意こそ
信心即生活の
根本であることを
忘れまい

OCTOBER 28

*Let's raise capable people on a broad scale
and prosper along with our members.*

広く人材を伸ばし
同志と共に
栄えよう

十月二十八日

OCTOBER 29

First, ponder well.
Then, act boldly.

まず思索せよ
次は大胆に動け

十月二十九日

OCTOBER 30

Let's discuss things in greater depth. Let's converse with a wider range of people. That is the basis from which to establish deep faith, our study of Buddhism and our daily lives, so we can sink roots in society.

対話を深めよう
対話を広めよう
そこから深い信心を
確立することだ
教学も生活も
そして社会に
根を張るためにも

十月三十日

President Ikeda meets with Count Coudenhove-Kalergi, 1967.

OCTOBER 31

Campaign cheerfully and spend an enjoyable day.

十月三十一日

朗らかに戦い
一日を楽しくおくれ

November

NOVEMBER 1

Let's tune up our organization regularly, so that it will run in the most effective way and no one will feel dissatisfied. Leaders should then carefully put each part in gear.

十一月一日

組織では常に
もっとも効果的で
誰も不満のない
完璧な整備をしよう
そして幹部は
緻密に一つ一つ
ギアを入れていこう

President Toda issues *Precepts for Youth*, 1951.

NOVEMBER 2

Welcome opinions, but silence slander.

十一月二日

意見はよく聞こう
しかし
誹謗は破折せよ

NOVEMBER 3

Let's do our utmost on the job and also make time enough to work for other people's happiness. This is 'enlightenment equals the nine worlds.'

己の職場では
全力をつくそう
そして時間を生み
利他に悠々と励もう
これが九界即仏界だ

十一月三日

Young Men's, Young Women's Divisions First General Meetings, Los Angeles, 1963.

NOVEMBER 4

No matter what happens in society, let's pursue our own course. Let those who laugh, laugh. Let those who slander us say what they will. Our road is a noble one and leads to a glorious future.

社会にいかなることがあっても

われわれはわが道を進もう

笑うものは笑え

貶すものは貶せ

われらの道は崇高にして

栄光ある未来につながるのだ

NOVEMBER 5

Make full use of your time, employ everyone available and visit all the members. That is the flowering of altruism. Only this unceasing effort will open a future as limitless as a vast plain.

十一月五日

あらゆる時間を利用し
あらゆる人々を活用して
家庭指導をやりぬこう
これが利他の展開だ
この一波万波のみが
未来を曠野のごとく
広げよう

NOVEMBER 6

Reform means action. Planning and discussion alone are pure theory and conservatism; they won't help you progress an inch. Let's move. Let's grasp the real situation and encourage people.

十一月六日

革新とは行動することだ
企画や話のみでは
一センチの前進もない
これは観念主義であり保守だ
動こう
そして実情をみきわめ
激励しぬいていこう

NOVEMBER 7

Let's hold enjoyable meetings that anyone can relate to and also put our full effort into individual guidance. Let's be courteous when giving guidance, so as not to create friction.

十一月七日

会合は愉しく
誰でも納得できるものにしよう
そして個人指導に
全力を尽くそう
指導にあっては
礼儀正しく
摩擦を起こさぬようにしよう

NOVEMBER 8

Before you complain, challenge the walls in front of you. This is the heroism of Kosen-rufu and the picture of human revolution.

十一月八日

愚痴をこぼすまえに
自分の前の壁に
挑戦することだ
これが広布の勇士であり
人間革命の姿である

Members must never cause accidents. One person's accident can undo a hundred people's efforts. Only sound, steady activities build solid organization.

十一月九日

同志はけっして
事故を起こしてはならぬ
百の努力も一人の事故で
水泡に帰してしまう
着実な活動のみが
磐石な体制を築くからだ

NOVEMBER 10

Let's live for the supreme purpose. From there, find a way of life meaningful to you. It will gush from the wellspring of a perfect Gongyo, morning and evening.

湧出される

五座三座の勤行から

その源泉は完璧な

生きがいを見つけよう

そこから自分らしい

生きゆこう

お互いに大目的に

十一月十日

NOVEMBER 11

Sound sleep and Daimoku every day are the source of enjoyable meetings, courageous action and absolute proof.

十一月十一日

熟睡とである

日々の題目と

その源泉は

厳然たる実証

勇気ある行動

愉しい会合

NOVEMBER 12

Let's pray earnestly about our own problems and desires. Undefeated by devils, let's also pray together for the advance of Kosen-rufu.

十一月十二日

自身の苦悩も願望も
真剣に祈ろう
さらに広布の進展も
皆で祈念しよう
断じて魔に負けずに

NOVEMBER 13

Before you complain, chant Daimoku.
Before you criticize, perfect yourself.
Before you torture yourself, talk with your seniors.
Before you worry, practice.

十一月十三日

愚痴をいうより題目だ
批判するより自身を磨け
悩んでいるより相談せよ
くよくよするより実践だ

NOVEMBER 14

Move positively. Talk positively, and speak positively. That is the key to advancing yourself — and the battle lines of Kosen-rufu — one more step.

十一月十四日

積極的に動け

そして

積極的に語れ　叫べ

それが自己も広布の戦線も

一歩前進する要諦だ

NOVEMBER 15

Progress toward any victory comes by joining together. It comes from unity — from absolutely nothing but unity.

なにはともあれ

勝利への前進は

スクラムを組むことだ

団結だ

団結しか絶対にない

十一月十五日

NOVEMBER 16

Win in small things. That is the basis of big victories.

まず小事に勝て
それが大事に勝つ
根本と知れ

十一月十六日

NOVEMBER 17

When it's time to be active, do your utmost. When it's time to relax, get a good rest. If you campaign without resting you'll exhaust yourself and achieve no results whatsoever.

十一月十七日

活躍する時には
大いに活躍しよう
休息をとる時は
ゆっくりと休息することだ
休息なき戦いは自らも疲れ
なんら効果を生まないからだ

NOVEMBER 18

*Let's forge on with great sincerity as sons
of the Gakkai, cherishing in our hearts the
single thought: 'We will hold our course.'
Let's inscribe the new and shining history of
Myoho in our own lives.*

十一月十八日

学会っ子は
〝わが道を行こう〟
の一言を胸に
大誠実をもって前進しよう
そしてわが肉団に輝く妙法の
新しき歴史を刻みゆこう

Soka Gakkai founded, 1930.
First President Tsunesaburo Makiguchi dies in prison, 1944.
First NSA seminar held at UCLA, 1968.

NOVEMBER 19

Always protect your members and respect them sincerely. Remember this attitude itself will quietly yet profoundly communicate your guidance and encouragement.

十一月十九日

ともかく相手を大切にし
尊敬することだ
その姿勢があってこそ
指導も激励も深く静かに
交流していくことを
忘れてはならない

NOVEMBER 20

Without sound sleep, you can't campaign.
The road to victory will open only when you
advance with fresh vitality.

熟睡しなければ
闘争はできない
生き生きとした
生命力の前進のみに
勝利という道が
開けるのだ

十一月二十日

NOVEMBER 21

It is completely against Buddhism to think everything will somehow come out all right just because you practice. It is precisely because you practice that you should recognize harsh realities for what they are. Organize your life and activities in a rational, scientific way and then aim for perfection.

信心しているから
なんとかなるとの考えは
大謗法である
信心していればこそ
厳しい現実を見極め
合理的　科学的に
生活や事業を組み立て
完璧を期することだ

NOVEMBER 22

Pay attention even to small details, such as being on time, choosing your words carefully, being courteous and so on. A leader's concern — or lack of it — has a vast influence on the entire membership.

十一月二十二日

小さいことにも
気をつけよう
たとえば時間の厳守
言葉遣い　礼儀等
幹部の心づかいの善し悪しが
全体に大きく影響を
与えるからである

First America group pilgrimage arrives Daisekiji, 1961.

NOVEMBER 23

A good plan, a job well done.

良い工夫を
良き仕事を

十一月二十三日

Buddhism is a struggle between the power of Buddha and the stern reality of devils. Remember that enlightenment, the basis of faith, lies in courageous action to surmount and crush these devils.

十一月二十四日

仏法は現実の魔と
仏との戦いである
ゆえに成仏という信心の根本は
これらの魔をのり越え
打ち破っていくところの
勇気ある行動のなかに
あることを忘れまい

NOVEMBER 25

Be aware of the family situation in each home used as a center for activities. Let's avoid causing them trouble and be sure to end meetings on time.

十一月二十五日

いかなる場合でも
それぞれの拠点になっている
家庭を理解し
迷惑をかけぬよう
会合も時間内で
終わらせよう

NOVEMBER 26

No matter what unpleasantness or humiliation we may meet, we are sons of the Gakkai. Those who stand firm in their faith will, in the long run, lead lives that are full, rewarding and without regret.

十一月二十六日

嫌なことも

悔しいことがあっても

われらは学会っ子だ

不退転の信心あるものは

最後はかならず悔いない

桜花爛漫の境涯を

つかむであろう

NOVEMBER 27

Let's take good care of our juniors with tolerance and understanding as broad as the sea. That is Buddhism of the people.

後輩を大切にしよう
それが民衆仏法である
海のような
包容力をもって

十一月二十七日

We should not be arrogant, show off,
overreach ourselves or be condescending. Let's
make still further progress today with strong
faith like the current of a mighty river.

十一月二十八日

驕（おご）りもせず

見栄もはらず

背伸びもせず

たかぶらず

大河の流れゆくがごとき

強靱（きょうじん）なる信仰で

今日もなんらかの前進をしよう

Let's shake hands with each of our members. Let's clap them on the shoulder and encourage them. Let's toil with all our might like workmen in overalls. We must never forget the Soka Gakkai's first stand as an ally of the people.

十一月二十九日

会員一人ひとりと
握手しよう
肩をたたき激励しよう
なっぱ服を着た気持ちで尽くそう
ともかく民衆の味方という
本来の学会の姿勢を
われらは永遠に
忘れてはならない

NOVEMBER 30

Let's greet our friends sincerely and encourage each other, even with just a single word. This warm, heartfelt rapport will strengthen discussion meetings, for it is the first step in creating staunch unity.

十一月三十日

わが友には一言でも
声をかけ激励しあおう
この温かい心の感応が
座談会を盛り上げ
強靱なスクラムを組む
第一歩だからである

December

DECEMBER 1

Let's successfully settle this year's accounts, in both our social and personal affairs. This is the only road to victory in the coming year.

十二月一日

この一年の総決算を
公私ともに
見事にやりぬこう
これこそ来年の
勝利に通ずる唯一の道だ

DECEMBER 2

If one can't manage his own family
satisfactorily, how can he lead anyone else?
Let's build families that will inspire trust.

わが家庭を
満足に治められない人が
なんで他の人々を
指導できようか
ともかく
信頼される家庭を
つくることだ

十二月二日

President Ikeda leaves for People's Republic of China, 1974.

DECEMBER 3

The symptoms of recession are appearing worldwide. Nevertheless, let's each chant Daimoku and, with a strong sense of economy, create lives of glory.

十二月三日

世界的に不況の兆候が
あらわれている
だが各自は題目をあげ
経済観念を強くもって
栄光の人生を築いていこう

DECEMBER 4

Each of you, fight for all you're worth. Be confident that he who fights will reap the greatest benefit. With iron unity, let's show the world the hidden strength of the Gakkai, leaving nothing to regret throughout our lives.

十二月四日

おのおのの全力を出して戦いぬこう

戦う者に

大功徳があることを確信し

悔いを生涯に残すな

そして学会の底力を

天下に示そう

鉄の団結をもって

DECEMBER 5

The road to human revolution equals our Buddhist movement, which permeates society through families and individuals. Never forget that it must start from discussion meetings.

十二月五日

個人も家庭も
社会に浸透する
仏法運動 即 人間革命への道は
絶対に座談会を起点とすることを
けっして忘れまい

President Ikeda completes *Ode to Youth*, 1970.

DECEMBER 6

The public is eager to find out about the Gakkai. Let's herald our movement freely. This too is Shakubuku of Jun'en Kofu, or the spread of Buddhism among people already open to its teachings.

民衆は学会を
知りたがっている
われらは伸びのびと
大いに学会を
宣揚していこう
これも順縁広布の折伏だ

十二月六日

DECEMBER 7

Let's carry ourselves proudly, as the children of revolution in a new era. With perseverance and sincerity, let's make friends of our neighbors and the general public.

誇り高く
新時代の革命児として
互いに振る舞おう
そして隣人と民衆を
忍耐と真心で
わが味方にしていこう

十二月七日

DECEMBER 8

You should wholeheartedly respect those pioneers who are your elders in faith, even if they do not presently hold a position. Treat them with utmost courtesy. That is the correct attitude for juniors.

十二月八日

たとえ今は役職がなくても
信心の先輩に対しては
心より尊敬し大切に
礼を踏むことが
後輩の正しい道である

DECEMBER 9

Don't hesitate. Jump in anywhere, speak boldly to anyone, in order to build a firm foundation for Kosen-rufu.

十二月九日

逡巡することなく
いかなる人
いかなる所にも
勇んでとびこもう
広布の磐石な布石のために

DECEMBER 10

Work at a reasonably rapid pace. That is the source of victory.

十二月十日

仕事は合理的迅速に
それが
勝利の源泉である

DECEMBER 11

Be warm to the people you encounter, both inside and outside our organization.

人と接する場合は
内外ともにあたたかく

十二月十一日

DECEMBER 12

Daimoku is the wellspring of life-functions. Life itself is the driving force of both daily existence and the workings of society, and that force is accelerated by the study of Buddhism.

十二月十二日

題目こそ
生命活動の源泉であり
その生命は
生活　社会活動の
推進力だ
その加速度を増すのが
教学である

DECEMBER 13

Let's bring up more and more capable people in our districts. At the same time, let's sink roots in society and together, enjoy studying the penetrating doctrines of Buddhism.

十二月十三日

いよいよブロックの人材の
構築を完璧にしていこう
社会に根を張りつつ
仲良く楽しく
鋭い教学の
研鑽をしながら

DECEMBER 14

*Let's speak courteously to all our members
and treat them kindly. Emotionalism or harsh
words can never convey real guidance.*

十二月十四日

会員には
言葉遣いをていねいに
そして親切に接しよう
感情や暴言で
けっして真の指導は
できないからだ

DECEMBER 15

Attending discussion meetings is the practice of Buddhism. However, during the final, hectic month of December, you should also pour your full effort into your own work, understanding that this is the practice of Buddhism, too.

十二月十五日

会合に出席することが
仏道修行ではあるが
また多忙な師走に
各々の道に精を出し
奔走することも
仏道修行であることを
理解すべきだ

DECEMBER 16

Whatever the campaign, whatever the activity, leaders should take the initiative and fight. With this in mind, let's get off to a running start.

十二月十六日

いかなる戦いも
いかなる活動も
幹部が絶対に率先して
戦おうではないか
その助走を開始しよう

DECEMBER 17

Let's broaden our contacts with the world and sink roots deep in society with guts and a smile, and an admirable display of capability.

十二月十七日

思いきり外部と接しよう
思いきり社会のなかに
笑顔と根性で根を張ろう
堂々たる実力を示しつつ

DECEMBER 18

*Let's bring back the fresh, earnest attitude
we had as new members. Listen to others'
personal experiences and freely relate your
own. This is the absolute confidence of faith.*

十二月十八日

これからは再び初信に戻り
体験を聞き
体験を大いに語っていこう
これこそ信仰の
絶対的確信であるからだ

DECEMBER 19

*Above all, let's speak courteously. Re-
member that since people are creatures of
feeling, words which convey acceptance and
understanding are expressions of mercy (Jihi).*

第一にも第二にも
言葉遣いを丁重にしよう
人は感情の動物であるがゆえに
包容性のある言葉こそ
慈悲の発露であることを
忘れまい

十二月十九日

DECEMBER 20

Whether you've won or lost, advance
cheerfully toward the next target.

たとえ勝っても負けても

朗らかに

次の目標に向かって進もう

十二月二十日

DECEMBER 21

Reorganize your work in perfect order.

仕事の
整理整頓を
完全に

十二月二十一日

DECEMBER 22

Today, once again, win cheerfully in society. Today, once again, devote yourself with deep faith to the Buddhist practice.

十二月二十二日

今日も朗らかに
社会のなかで勝利する一日を
今日も深き信仰で
仏道修行といわれる一日を

DECEMBER 23

Learn to understand the times, and study everything you can.

十二月二十三日

時代感覚を身につけよ
そして
あらゆるものを
勉強していこう

DECEMBER 24

*Be warm and patient when giving guid-
ance. Never be emotional. These are key points
to remember when visiting members.*
*Also, let's bring the year to a victorious
conclusion.*

十二月二十四日

指導は忍耐強く

あたたかく行おう

けっして感情的になってはならない

これが家庭指導の枢要である

そして本年の有終の美を飾ろう

DECEMBER 25

Make the first move. Don't take the defensive.

先手を打て
後手になるな

十二月二十五日

DECEMBER 26

Cool judgment.
Quick action.

冷静なる判断
敏速なる処置

十二月二十六日

DECEMBER 27

Important things should be communicated without delay. Then, whatever the problem, let's resolve it successfully.

大事な要件は

火急に連絡しあうこと

そしていかなる事件も

立派に解決していこう

十二月二十七日

DECEMBER 28

Leaders should advance on their own initiative and receive training. They should also take great pains in raising their juniors. Unless leaders build a foundation, the members cannot advance hopefully. Training, with the aim of bringing up capable people, is the chief essential in further developing the Gakkai.

十二月二十八日

幹部は自ら進んで教育を受け

後輩をまた懇切に教育していこう

基礎　基本をつくらずして

全員の希望あふるる前進はない

人材育成のための教育——

これが再び学会を築き上げる

最大の要件なのだ

Openly state your own opinions, and be
equally open to the opinions of other people.

率直に
意見をいえ
率直に
意見を聞け

十二月二十九日

DECEMBER 30

Let's advance each day without any accidents. Let's use good common sense and take constructive action in all areas.

十二月三十日

日々事故なく
そして常識豊かに
すべて価値的な行動で
前進しよう

DECEMBER 31

Thank you very much for all your efforts this year. Next year, let's again forge boldly ahead, clearing the road, seeking the noblest way of life and sharing it with other people.

十二月三十一日

本年一年
本当にご苦労さまでした
来年こそ再び
開道者の道を
知道者の道を
そして説道者の道を
凛然と進んでいこう